25 CYCLE ROUTES

In and Around

GLASGOW

Erl B. Wilkie

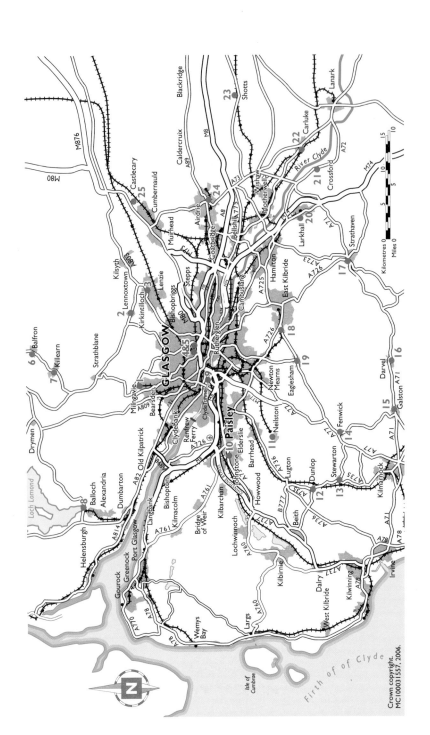

Crown copyright.
MC100031557, 2006.

25 CYCLE ROUTES

In and Around

GLASGOW

Erl B. Wilkie

MERCAT PRESS

First edition published in 1996 by HMSO
Second edition published in 2006 by Mercat Press
at 10 Coates Crescent, Edinburgh EH3 7AL
www.mercatpress.com

ISBN-13: 978-1-84183-095-7
ISBN-10: 1-84183-095-X

Also available in this series:
25 Cycle Routes—Edinburgh and Lothian
25 Cycle Routes—Stirling and the Trossachs
25 Cycle Routes—Kingdom of Fife
25 Cycle Routes—Argyll and Bute

Printed and bound in Great Britain by Bell & Bain Ltd

CONTENTS

FOREWORD BY CTC

Cycling is healthy, environmentally-friendly—and above all fun! Travel at your own pace, meet people along the way and experience the real country. Explore parts of the country that you didn't know existed—and improve your fitness at the same time! Cycling is good for you, so go by bike, and you'll feel a whole lot better for it.

Safety considerations and equipment needed

- Before you go cycling, check your bike thoroughly for broken, worn and/or loose parts. In particular, check for worn tyres and broken/loose spokes. Ensure that both brakes and the gear system are working well, with the chain lightly oiled and running smoothly. If in doubt your local bike shop will advise you further. Better to fix things now, than to spoil your ride later.

- Carry a cycle lock and key, and a small tool kit (spare inner tube, tyre levers, small adjustable spanner, puncture repair outfit, pump and Allen keys if your bike needs them).

- If you are really loading up for a big adventure, your luggage should be on the bike, not your back. A rear carrying rack is useful. Ideally pack everything into plastic bags inside a saddlebag or panniers properly secured to this rack. Check your load is balanced, and the weight doesn't affect the steering/handling of the bike. If you prefer to travel light, you can fit most things into a bumbag.

- Always carry food and water/liquid. Cyclists are advised to drink little and often.

- Comfortable clothing is essential. For colder days wear two or three layers: you can take them off once you've warmed up and put them on if you cool off. Wet-weather gear is useful if you've

METRIC MEASUREMENTS

At the beginning of each route, the distance is given in miles and kilometres. Within the text, all measurements are metric for simplicity (and indeed our Ordnance Survey maps are now all metric). However, it was felt that a conversion table might be useful to those readers who, like the author, still tend to think in miles.

The basic statistic to remember is that one kilometre is five-eighths of a mile. Half a mile is equivalent to 800 metres and a quarter-mile is 400 metres. Below that distance, yards and metres are little different in practical terms.

km	miles
1	0.625
1.6	1
2	1.25
3	1.875
3.2	2
4	2.5
4.8	3
5	3.125
6	3.75
6.4	4
7	4.375
8	5
9	5.625
10	6.25
16	10

got the space to carry it. For hot weather don't forget your sun cream and shades.

- You don't have to wear specialist cycle clothing to enjoy cycling. Padded shorts, gloves, cycling shoes, cycle helmets and much more can be purchased at cycle shops if you are interested. NB: it is not compulsory to wear a helmet, and the choice is yours. CTC can provide further information on helmets if needed.

- Check your riding position is comfortable. Saddle height: when seated, place your heel on the pedal when it is at its lowest point. Your leg should be straight, and your knee just off the locked position. On the subject of riding comfort, many bikes are supplied with saddles designed for men (long and narrow). Women may prefer to sit on a saddle designed for women (shorter and wider at the back). These are available from bike shops.

- There is some useful information for cyclists in the *Highway Code*. This is available from garages, bookshops or your local library.

- If you think that you may be cycling when it is dark, you will need to fit front and rear lights. (This is a legal requirement.) Lights and reflectors/reflective clothing are also useful in bad weather conditions.

- In the event of an accident, it is advisable to note the time and place of the incident, the names and addresses of those involved, details of their insurance company, and vehicle registration numbers and details of any witnesses. In the event of injury or damage, report the incident to the police immediately.

 For further information about cycling...

CTC (Cyclists' Touring Club) is Britain's largest cycling organisation, and can provide a wealth of information and advice about all aspects of cycling. CTC works on behalf of all cyclists to promote cycling and to protect cyclists' interests.

Membership includes free third-party insurance, legal aid, touring and technical information, a bi-monthly magazine, *Cycle*, and many other resources.

For further details contact CTC at: Parklands, Railton Road, Guildford, Surrey GU2 9JX; or telephone the Cyclists' Helpline, 0870 8730060; or e-mail cycling@ctc.org.uk; or visit the website: www.ctc.org.uk.

INTRODUCTION

In this second edition the philosophy of this book has not changed: it still contains 25 cycle routes around Glasgow covering a complete 360-degree radius around the city, with connections into the city at various locations. Each of the routes is interlinked, except Routes 9 and 25, but even in these locations the routes are connected by two areas of linear, cycleable pathways. The routes vary in length from 14.5 km (9 miles) to 50 km (31 miles) and in difficulty from easy to very demanding. Owing to the geography of west central Scotland, it is impossible to find any length of totally flat terrain, therefore even the easiest routes in this book have small hilly stretches.

As with other books in the series, it adopts two principles. The first is to encourage those who are new to cycling and those who haven't ridden a bike for a long time, or even those who just think they might like cycling, to go out and do it. Secondly, the aim is to allow the reader to be able to travel to the beginning of as many routes as possible using public transport. As a result, 15 of the routes start and end at railway stations, with some passing other stations en route, allowing the reader great flexibility in choosing what distance to cycle.

For the most part the routes use the network of minor roads, with negligible vehicular traffic flows, which are so abundant in this part of the world and therefore ideal for cycling. Indeed, since the first edition of this book was published, some councils have signed these routes, thus identifying them as official cycle routes in their area. Many of the routes also connect with, and use, lengths of the existing network of designated cycle routes such as Sustrans National Cycle Network or the Forth and Clyde Canal tow path. There are no particularly difficult surfaces to negotiate along these routes, although some short distances of off-road stretches can be muddy in wet weather, and sometimes the path can be narrow.

It is completely legal to cycle on all of these routes in their entirety, so no opposition to cycling should be encountered. There are one or two locations where to be absolutely on the safe side I have recommended that the cyclist dismount, but this is in the interest of safety or manoeuverability, not legality. On occasion some of the routes use A- and B-class roads for short distances, but I have avoided using very busy roads and have only recommended a route along a stretch of A- or B-class road when I felt it was safe enough to do so. However readers must make their own judgement about safety depending on the circumstances prevailing at the time. If in doubt, do not attempt it!

I hope you will enjoy these routes, which pass through a very varied terrain and which I feel show the area around Scotland's largest city at its scenic best.

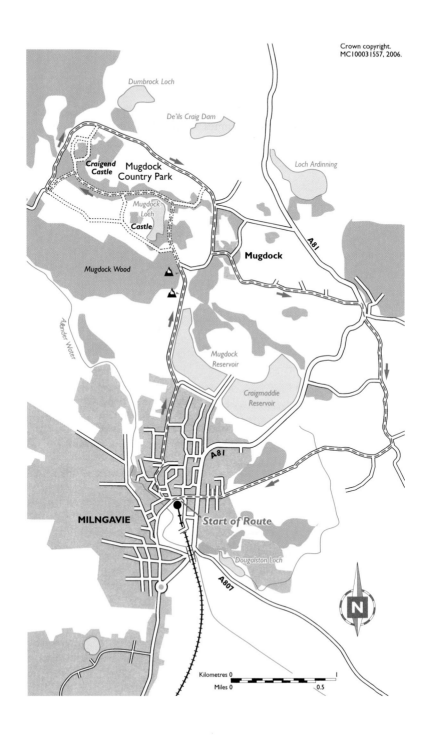

Crown copyright.
MC100031557, 2006.

MILNGAVIE TO MUGDOCK COUNTRY PARK

L eave the car park at Milngavie Railway Station and turn left along Station Road for about 100m, taking care along this stretch of busy dual carriageway, and turn right into Ellangowan Road, which later becomes Mugdock Road. If the reader is travelling by car to the beginning of the route, then there are convenient car parks near the junction of Station Road and Ellangowan Road.

Follow this road for just over 1.5 km, climbing all the time, passing en route Mugdock and Craigmaddie Reservoirs, to where Mugdock Road makes a U-turn up a steep gradient. At this point the access road to Mugdock Country Park begins straight on, just as Mugdock Road begins its sharp turn, and continues for a short distance to South Lodge car park.

The Mugdock and Craigmaddie Reservoirs, known as Glasgow's Water Works, were built in the middle of the nineteenth century as holding reservoirs for Glasgow's water supply, which was

INFORMATION

Distance: 14.5 km (9 miles), circular route.

Map: OS Landranger, sheet 64.

Start and finish: Milngavie Railway Station car park.

Terrain: Hilly with short stretches of steep gradients.

Refreshments: Mugdock Visitors' Centre.

Mugdock Castle.

piped from Loch Katrine. Queen Victoria turned the wheel that first opened the valve to send this water through the pipes to Milngavie on 14 October 1859.

South Lodge Car Park at the entrance to Mugdock Country Park is an ideal start to the route for those wishing to miss out the fairly steep gradients encountered in the first 1.5 km or so, which, incidentally, is the hilliest part of this route. I would point out, though, that the car park has only space for a small number of cars.

Mugdock Country Park was opened in 1982, and was one of the first of its kind to be opened in Central Scotland. It contains many interesting features and places such as Mugdock Castle, which dates back to the thirteenth century, built by Sir David de Grahame. It belonged to the famous Graham family who have featured so prominently in Scottish history, with only short interruptions, until the twentieth century.

Other places of interest are Moothill, possibly the site of an ancient crannog and a medieval Hill

Ruins of Craigend Castle.

of Judgement; Gallowhill, which until 1718 was the local place of execution; and Craigend Castle. Craigend Castle was designed by James Smith of Jordanhill in 1818 for the Smith family, Lairds of Craigend, who had purchased the land from the Grahams in 1670. The last laird died in 1851 and the estate was passed to Sir Andrew Buchanan, ambassador to the Viennese Court. In this century it was occupied by Sir Harold Yarrow, the Clyde shipbuilder, and George Outram, one of the owners of the *Glasgow Herald* newspaper (now *The Herald*). The house and land were sold to the Wilson family in 1946, who owned a zoo in Glasgow, and in 1949 Craigend Zoo opened to the public. It was not a success, however, for it closed 6 years later.

A short distance after entering the park, a T-junction is reached. Turn right here, and after a further few metres turn right again over a small bridge and continue along this road past Mugdock Loch, the home of many varieties of water fowl, at the other side of which stand the ruins of Mugdock Castle. Continue along this road to another T-junction, where the route continues to the left along an avenue lined by willow and birch to the remnants of Craigend Castle. Just a few metres before this castle is reached, take the road to the left which winds across moorland to the Khyber Pass car park. Stop here and look to the west, where you will see, on a fine day, a breathtaking view over Glasgow and the Clyde Valley.

Here, leave Mugdock Country Park at the exit by Khyber Pass car park and turn right on to the minor road. After a short downhill stretch the cyclist will have to start climbing again, but thankfully not for long, for after a few hundred metres the top of the hill is reached. Within 1.5 km or so a road junction is reached. Pass this and continue on to a second junction and turn left and on through Mugdock Village, after which it soon joins the A81. Turn right on to this busy road for about 300m and then turn left on to the minor road at the next junction. Almost immediately, turn right again on to the road which is signed for Balmore. Carry on along this road for 1.5 km to another junction, and here turn right, at the old parish church, down a hill. After 200m turn right again. Follow this road down past Dougalston Golf Club to the controlled junction with the A81, carry straight on, and in just over 100m Milngavie Railway Station is to be found on the left.

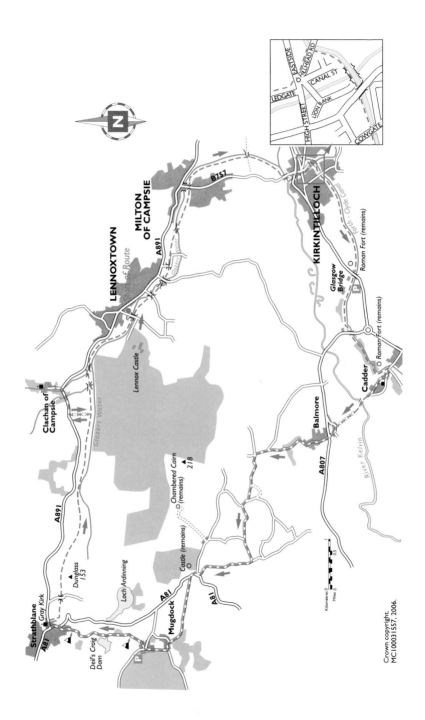

LENNOXTOWN TO STRATHBLANE

The village of Lennoxtown, previously known as Newton of Campsie, was once noted for calico printing and handloom weaving, but nowadays these industries have completely vanished. The village is now mainly a residential area for Kirkintilloch and Glasgow. However, Lennoxtown is also a place where cyclists can gain access to the Campsie Hills.

This route starts at the car park at the junction of Station Road and Main Street, Lennoxtown. Follow Station Road first down a slight incline to where a bridge crosses over the pathway, which uses the track bed of the former Kirkintilloch to Gartness railway. As the name of the road suggests, this was the site of Lennoxtown Railway Station. Just before crossing this bridge, turn right down a steep and rough ramp which goes from road level to the path. At the bottom of this ramp turn left, and begin cycling along this sheltered tree-lined track towards Kirkintilloch. After some 3 km the route passes Milton of Campsie, another village with much the same history as Lennoxtown, although in the eighteenth century its claim to fame was as a centre for whisky smuggling. From Milton of Campsie it is about 1.5 km along a pleasant wooded path to Kirkintilloch, where the footpath joins the Kilsyth Road. The cyclist should cross Kilsyth Road and then continue by way of the path adjacent to Ledgate, across the Hillhead Roundabout and onto Hillhead Road, turning right at the top of this onto the Forth and Clyde Canal, where the route continues westward.

Kirkintilloch originated as *Caerpentulach*, meaning 'the fort on the ridge'. This fort would have been part of the Antonine Wall. From the twelfth century this area was in the hands of the Comyn family, who had their castle at Kirkintilloch. The mote of the castle is still visible at Peel

INFORMATION

Distance: 32.2 km (20 miles), circular route.

Map: OS Landranger, sheet 64.

Start and finish: Station Road car park, Lennoxtown.

Terrain: Mainly flat for 20.9 km (13.0 miles) then generally undulating. The short off-road stretch can be muddy in wet weather.

Refreshments: Various places in Kirkintilloch. The Stables Restaurant and Bar, Glasgow Road Bridge, just west of Kirkintilloch. The Coach House, Balmore. Tower Road, Aldessan Art Gallery coffee shop, Clachan of Campsie. Kirkhouse Inn, Strathblane.

Park. Kirkintilloch is an ancient town which was granted Burgal status by William Comyn in 1211. The Barony was transferred to the Flemings by Robert the Bruce after the Battle of Bannockburn (1314).

Kirkintilloch remained a small, predominantly agricultural and weaving community, until the advent of the Forth and Clyde Canal. It would be true to say that the town we know today owes much of its development to the canal. In 1773, while work had stopped on the canal further west, Kirkintilloch was operating as Scotland's first inland port, providing access from the River Forth to the east. In 1860 the first shipbuilding and repair yard was opened there, and shipbuilding went on in Kirkintilloch until the Second World War. There were also iron foundries located in the town because of the relatively cheap transportation of pig iron along this waterway.

The Stables.

Continue along the canal tow path to Glasgow Bridge, where refreshments can be had at the Stables Restaurant and Bar. This fine Georgian building was converted to its present use in 1981, but as its name suggests, it was once the stables where the horses needed for towing the barges were kept. At the time of its restoration, boats also returned to the canal. Some pleasure boats operate from here, and in the summer ply up and down the canal.

Another 1.5 km or so further on is Cadder Church, which was a poaching ground of bodysnatchers who supplied the medical profession of the early nineteenth century with bodies for experiments in anatomy. Because of its close proximity to the canal, Cadder Church was an ideal spot for body-snatching, the canal being a fast and convenient way to transport the bodies to both Edinburgh and Glasgow as the need required. Indeed, this happened so often that the people of Cadder had a watch-house built, and used iron mort-safes to protect their dead from attack. These can still be seen in the churchyard today.

At Cadder Church turn right, away from the tow path, and take the road by the side of the church. There is a sign which states that this road is for authorised vehicles only. However, this is a right of way, and so can be used by pedestrians and cyclists. Follow this road for 400m or so, at which point a

Cadder Parish Church.

junction is reached. Here follow the path between the seventeenth and eighteenth holes of the Kier Golf Course, which is one of the two courses of the Cawder Golf Club.

After passing through the golf course, cross the River Kelvin by the footbridge. Continue along this path for a short distance to where it turns at right angles, after which it continues for the remaining 400m to Balmore. Somewhere along this stretch of road the Antonine Wall would have crossed at right angles, but, alas, there is no trace of it left in the vicinity. At the end of this path turn left and follow the road around, passing the lower part of Balmore village, to the junction of the A807. Here cross this road, carefully, and continue through the upper part of Balmore village to a junction, at which point take the right hand road and carry on for about 1.5 km to the fourway junction with Tower Road. Turn left along Tower Road and continue for about 2.5 km to a T-junction. Here turn right and follow this road to the junction with the A81, then turn right and ride along this busy road for about 300m to the junction with the minor road to Mugdock on the left. Continue along this road to the village of Mugdock.

Just after the village a T-junction is reached. Turn right here and follow this road for 300m only, to yet another junction, and here take the minor road signposted to Strathblane. This road, which is called Old Mugdock Road, passes Deils Craig Dam before descending the steep hill into Strathblane. On reaching the T-junction, turn right onto Dumbrock Road, at the end of which is the junction with the A81 (Glasgow to Aberfoyle Road). Here turn left and continue for approximately 15m to the A891 (Strathblane to Lennoxtown Road). Turn right onto this road and travel in the direction of Lennoxtown for 30m or so. Here on the right a path begins, which is signposted, connecting, once again, to the cycleway on the disused Gartness to Kirkintilloch railway line. At the beginning of this path take care when crossing the timber drainage channels, as some are above the surface level of the path and can be slippy.

Just before starting down this path, stop awhile at the old Gray Kirk, for the memories of many historical happenings haunt these hallowed grounds. The present church dates from 1803, being built on the same site as a much earlier kirk, within which Mary, Countess of Angus, daughter of Robert III and sister of James I, lies buried. There is an ancient weatherbeaten stone within the churchyard which is thought to be a Roman waymarker, and which is similar to others in various locations around the area.

Old church bell at Clachan of Campsie.

Once on the pathway, continue on for 8 km to get back to the point where the route began at Lennoxtown. After about 6.4 km a junction with another path is reached, which is signposted to Clachan of Campsie. It is worth the 800m detour to visit this place, for it is now a craft village with a collection of small businesses which are open to the public. These include painting and picture framing, guitar and violin making and the Aldessan Art Gallery with its fine coffee shop. Last, but certainly not least for the cyclist, there is also a very fine bike shop.

Cycle shop at Clachan of Campsie.

The ninth-century saint, Saint Machan, who was said to be one of the first native-born Evangelists, built the first place of worship in the area of Clachan of Campsie. In 1175 a church was built on the site of his grave. After the Reformation another church was built in its place. Finally, when the High Church was built in the nineteenth century, the old church was allowed to fall into disrepair and only a gable is left standing. During the village's face-lift in 1993, the old kirk bell, with the date 1729 inscribed upon it, was put on display in the village square. In the graveyard there is the old Mausoleum of the Lennox family dating back many centuries. Other interesting people are also buried there, such as John Bell, the Court Physician to the Russian Tsar Peter the Great, and William Boick, Covenanter and martyr.

Once back on to the cycleway, a little further towards Lennoxtown, you pass Lennox Castle, which was the seat of the Lennox family until 1927, when it was sold and developed as a psychiatric hospital.

Just as the cycleway reaches the village you will come to the second bridge over the path (the first being at Lennox Castle). Climb to the road above, turn left and follow the road back to the car park.

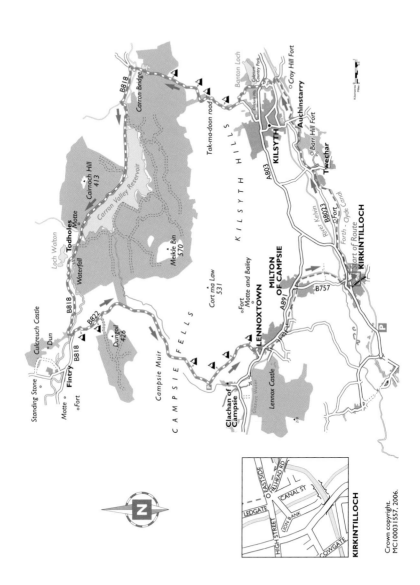

Crown copyright.
MC100031557, 2006.

KIRKINTILLOCH TO THE CAMPSIE HILLS

The route begins at the car park at Townhead in Kirkintilloch, by the tow-path of the Forth and Clyde Canal, which forms the first 9.7 km of this route. The Forth and Clyde Canal follows roughly the same route as the Antonine Wall; the reason for this is simply that it is the shortest distance between the east and west coasts of Scotland.

Before the Forth and Clyde Canal was built, ships wishing to get from the west coast to the east would have had to sail round the top of Scotland: a distance in excess of 300 miles and a very arduous and dangerous journey, especially in rough weather. The proposed line of the canal on the other hand was only 35 miles long. Digging began at Grangemouth on the River Forth in 1768 and it took 22 years to complete, finishing at Bowling on the River Clyde in 1790, where the company chairman poured a hogshead of Forth water into the Clyde.

Begin along the tow-path of the canal, heading east to Twechar. Here the tow-path passes close to Barr Hill and Croy Hill, which have a Roman fort on each. This area possesses the best stretches of the Antonine Wall to be seen within a short distance from the canal. These Roman remains are easily accessible. Leave the tow-path and cross over the canal at the bridge which carries the road into the village of Twechar. Keep to the left side of the road for about 100m, then you will see a track going off to the left. Take this for 400m up a long hill until a covered circular concrete reservoir is reached, then take the path to the left, through a gate and on another 50m to Barr Hill Fort. From here there is a very good view of the canal and the surrounding countryside below.

INFORMATION

Distance: 48.3 km (30 miles), circular route.

Map: OS Landranger, sheet 64 and 57.

Start and finish: Townhead car park, Kirkintilloch.

Terrain: This route is a long distance with some very long steep hills, and is not recommended for children. The worst hill is the Tak-ma-doon Road, which ascends 263 m in 4.8 km (3.0 miles) with short stretches of up to 1 in 7 gradients. However, the stretch along the Forth and Clyde Canal is flat and this part of the route can be tackled by everyone. Indeed, this 9.7 km (6.0 miles) out/9.7 km (6.0 miles) back route could be used in its own right.

Refreshments: Various places in Kirkintilloch, Kilsyth, Lennoxtown and Fintry. The Carron Bridge Hotel, Carron Bridge.

Cyclists—and swans—on the canal.

After returning to the tow-path at Twechar, continue east, and very soon Auchinstarry is reached. The canal passes under the B802 (the Kilsyth to Cumbernauld Road) at Auchinstarry, and is spanned by a non-opening bascule bridge. Some 300m away in the direction of Kilsyth is a disused quarry, which has been turned into a leisure area by the local Council. The floor of the quarry is under water, forming a small loch surrounded by landscaped areas in the foreground with the backdrop of the 30.5 m high whinstone face exposed behind. This is also worth a visit, and, as there is a picnic area, it is an ideal spot for a welcome break.

Carry on for about another 2.5 km to Craigmalloch, where the canal crosses the road to Dullatur. This is where the main source of water enters the canal, the inlet being right beside the road and running in a lade from Banton Loch 1.5 km away to the north.

From here turn left and continue north on this minor road for about 800m, to the A803, the Kilsyth to Falkirk Road. On reaching the A803 turn left and follow this road for about 400m, taking care here, for it can be busy. Then turn right into Colzium Country Park, the entrance of which is signposted. On entering the park, carry on along the road for another 400m to Colzium House. If you want to visit Banton Loch, it can be reached by turning right on to a track just before the park car park is reached.

The Battle of Kilsyth (1645), which took place during the Civil War, was fought in the area where

Banton Loch now exists. It was a resounding victory for the Marquis of Montrose with his army of Highlanders, who fought on the side of Charles I against the Covenanter government of the time. Here we find such names as Slaughter Howe, Bullet Knowe and Drum Burn, testifying to the ferocity of this battle.

The Clock Theatre at Colzium House.

Colzium House, formerly the 19th-century seat of the Edmonstones of Duntreath, is now a museum. Go on past the Clock Theatre, once the stables, to join the Tak-ma-doon Road 200m further on. Once on the Tak-ma-doon Road, the ascent into the Kilsyth Hills begins.

Stop at the top of this long hill to see the spectacular view over nearly the whole of the Forth and Clyde valley. After the exertion of the climb, a break at this time will be most welcome. It is

Colzium Park.

also worth pointing out that for those who want to do the cycle run along the road at the top of the Campsie Fells, therefore missing out the rigours of the Tak-ma-doon Road, this is where to begin, as the viewpoint has space for about 20 cars. From here it is possible to cycle some 16 km to Fintry and back without encountering any major hills, although the route is not entirely flat.

From here on, the area through which this route passes is one of peace and tranquillity. It is almost like closing a door and leaving the world outside. It is difficult to imagine, while surrounded by such a vast area of unspoilt beauty, that it is only 24 km from the heart of Glasgow, and even less from Stirling.

Go along this unclassified road for 3.2 km, through the eastern extremity of Carron Valley Forest, to Carron Bridge, which was built in 1695 to replace a ford that had existed for many hundreds of years as part of the old drove road from Kilsyth to Stirling. This bridge looks larger than it needs to be, with its two span stone arches. This is because the River Carron was much larger before Loch Carron was dammed to make a reservoir.

From here turn left on to the B818. At this point you will encounter the Carron Bridge Hotel, where sustenance can be had.

About 2.5 km along the B818 is the eastern entrance to the Carron Valley Forest, where an alternative route along forestry roads, skirting the south side of the reservoir, can be found. This route is very picturesque and well worth taking, although it adds a further 3.2 km and some more hills to the journey. However, the 6.4 km route along the B818 is also very attractive, with a better surface for cycling.

The routes once again converge at Todholes on the western side of the reservoir, and continue on another 5.6 km to the junction with the B822, passing first the Loup of Fintry, where the Endrick cascades over a height of upwards of 30m from the high moorland into the valley below.

On reaching the B822 it is barely 800m to the beginning of Fintry, a beautiful and sleepy little village with an ancient past. Back to the route. From where the B818 joins the B822 the road climbs another 150m in the next 5.6 km, which is of course a mere bagatelle for those cyclists who have recently climbed the Tak-ma-doon Road, although it's still another major hill. But thankfully it's the last, for once at the top of this hill the road begins a steady descent down to Lennoxtown.

Before the final 3.2 km descent down Crow Road to Lennoxtown, stop at the car park, where on a fine day there are wonderful views south over the Kelvin Valley to Glasgow itself and west to Loch Lomond and the Arrochar Alps beyond.

View of Ben Lomond from the route.

Take care going down the long straight incline on Crow Road, for high speeds can easily be achieved and there is a sharp corner to be negotiated at the bottom. At the end of Crow Road is the junction of the A891. Here cross, taking care, into Station Road. This is where the route from Lennoxtown to Strathblane (see Route 2) began. Continue, as Route 2, down Station Road and turn left on to the cycleway for the last, flat, 8 km back into Kirkintilloch.

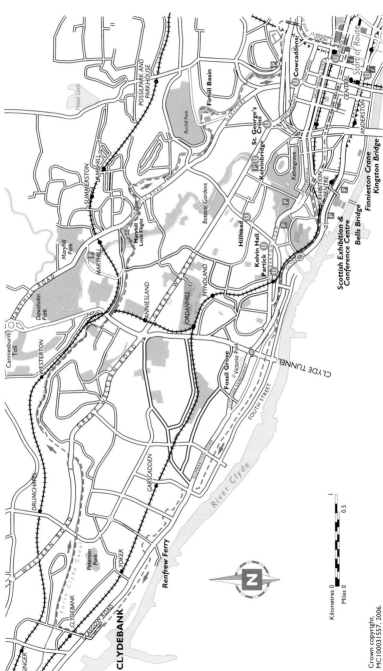

Crown copyright.
MC100031557. 2006.

GLASGOW CITY CENTRE TO CLYDEBANK

The route starts at the south side of George Square, which is dominated by the City Chambers at its east end, designed and built between 1883 and 1889 by William Young to represent, both outside and inside, the grandeur and opulence of this fine Victorian city.

Begin cycling along St Vincent Street for two blocks only and turn left onto the contra-flow cycle network in West Nile Street; continue right along Gordon Street, cross Union Street and go past the front of Central Station to Hope Street and turn left. Turn right at the next east/west street, which is Waterloo Street, and then left at the end of the next block into Wellington Street. Thereafter carry straight on over Argyle Street and turn right on to the National Cycle Route 75, which runs along the south footway/cycleway of Broomielaw and past the Finnieston Crane, which stands 53.4m above the River Clyde, to Bell's Bridge. This imposing city landmark was built in 1932, and had a lifting capacity of 162.5 tonnes. Latterly it was used only intermittently until it was decommissioned in 1994 and preserved as an industrial monument. In its heyday, however, it was in constant use lifting boilers and engines into ships that had recently been completed in the many shipyards of the upper Clyde. It was also used to lift the giant steam locomotives which were exported from Glasgow for use on railways all over the world.

This route is a clearly

INFORMATION

Distance: 24.1 km (15 miles), circular route.

Map: OS Landranger, sheet 64.

Start and finish: George Square, Glasgow or Queen Street Station.

Alternative start at Bell's Bridge: Just take the train to Exhibition Centre and follow the signed pedestrian/cycle route to the SECC.

Terrain: Generally flat.

Refreshments: Various places in Glasgow. Playdrome cafeteria, Clydebank. Lock 27, Forth and Clyde Canal, north of Anniesland Cross.

The famous Finnieston Crane.

signposted designated cycleway; therefore, it is not necessary to describe the route in detail but merely to point out the places of interest as they are passed. The Glasgow to Loch Lomond Cycleway beginning at Bell's Bridge was opened in 1989 and was the first long-distance cycleway in the west of Scotland. Its stretch of 34 km has proved popular as a safe off-road route for cyclists and pedestrians ever since. Bell's Bridge is also the junction of two other major long-distance cycle routes: the Glasgow to Irvine, Ardrossan and Greenock cycleway (opened fully in 1993) and the Glasgow to Edinburgh cycle route, which you have already been using for the last 2km. The latter is also the route of the Clyde Walkway to Strathclyde Park. On the other side of the river is the new headquarters of BBC Scotland, and immediately to its west is the Glasgow Science Centre with its many attractions, including a planetarium and Imax cinema.

Carry on past the Scottish Exhibition and Conference Centre, the Crowne Plaza Hotel and the footbridge which links this area with the Science Centre across the river. After crossing the Clydeside Expressway by the pedestrian footbridge at the SV *Glenlee*, Glasgow's own tall ship and very

The Armadillo—The Scottish Exhibition and Conference Centre.

much worth a visit, the route runs west, parallel to this road and the River Clyde passing the massive redevelopment of the Clydeside area known as Glasgow Harbour. At this point it should be noted that while the massive redevelopment is in progress this route is subject to diversion, but will always be open for cycling. When the development is complete the National Cycle Route will run along the riverside. After a further 2 km the route joins the track-bed of the former Lanarkshire/Dumbartonshire railway line from Partick through Whiteinch, Scotstoun and Yoker to Clydebank. There is a ramp down to Primrose Street in Scotstoun where there is easy access to Victoria Park, one of Glasgow's many beautiful parks. Built partly on the site of an old quarry, Victoria Park is renowned for its formal rock gardens and arboretum. Its most famous attraction is the Fossil Grove, uncovered in 1887, which is a unique geological example of petrified tree stumps and roots that grew some 250 million years ago.

Continuing on the route for a further 2.4 km, the cycleway passes close to the Renfrew Ferry at Yoker. This river crossing was served for many years by a car ferry between Yoker and Renfrew. The current ferry service, which started in 1984, caters only for pedestrians and cyclists as, since the opening of the Clyde Tunnel, there is no need to transport motor vehicles.

On entering Clydebank, the cycleway leaves the railway line and comes out on to Clyde Street. Here, follow the signs for Loch Lomond. The route carries on through an underpass under Glasgow Road and joins a path which runs parallel to Argyll Road for about 200m or so, to where it reaches the junction with Barns Street. This is the point at which the route leaves the cycleway. Take the street on the opposite side of this road, and within 100m the tow-path of the Forth and Clyde Canal is reached. Here turn right along the

Cyclists at Lock 27.

tow-path heading back in an easterly direction. (On the western side of Argyll Road is the Clydebank Playdrome, where refreshment can be found at its cafeteria.)

Once on the canal the route is again easy to follow. Continue along the tow-path for 6 km, passing en route Lock 27, a hostelry situated right on the canal tow-path, where refreshment can be had. Further on now to the Kelvin Aqueduct and Maryhill Lock Flight, to Stockingfield, where the main canal joins the Glasgow branch.

The Kelvin Aqueduct carries the canal 22.9m above the River Kelvin and is the largest structure on this canal. After the Kelvin Aqueduct has been crossed, the tow-path climbs through Maryhill Lock Flight. This is the highest part of the canal, the summit level being 47.5m above sea level.

Until recently the canal was bounded by factories manufacturing rubber products, oil by-products, a dye-works, grain mills and a distillery. In its heyday this part of the canal would have been bustling with barges and other traffic using the Glasgow branch to get to the wharves at Port Dundas. Sadly, much of this industry has now disappeared. However, this has been beneficial to the canal in other ways, because as the factories have stopped depositing harmful waste it can now support flora and fauna unknown for the last 150 years. You may be surprised by the many varieties of water fowl you encounter on the way along the canal. There are coots, moorhens, ducks and swans, all this before you even come to Ruchill.

Once Stockingfield junction is reached, the route continues east along the tow-path of the Glasgow branch back towards the city. After 2.4 km, passing along the length of Maryhill, the tow-path passes Firhill Stadium, the home of one of Glasgow's many famous football clubs—Partick Thistle.

On the left is Firhill Basin, which was built as a timber basin in 1788. Originally much larger, its purpose was to store logs until they were ready for use by the sawmills. After this point it can be seen that the canal is set quite high, affording a good view over the city centre.

From here it is about 1.6 km to Port Dundas, where the canal ends. As its name suggests, it was built as a port, taking its name from the first governor of the Canal Company, Sir Thomas Dundas. It was built at One Hundred Acre Hill, which was, at the time, above the city of Glasgow. Wharves, basins, granaries and warehouses were constructed. From its earliest days the canal was used extensively by passenger boats as the quickest and most comfortable way to get from Glasgow to Edinburgh and vice versa. In 1848 the Canal Company stopped its passenger service. By this time the Edinburgh to Glasgow railway had opened, and everyone wanted to travel by train. Other companies ran passenger services until 1876. Pleasure steamers were introduced in 1893 and only stopped at the beginning of the Second World War.

From where the canal ends the route continues right down Craighall Road almost to where it goes under the M8. Here there is a footpath which enters Sighthill Park, and after a short distance along this footpath Kyle Street footbridge is found. Cross this footpath into Kyle Street, turn right into Baird Street and then carry straight on at the traffic lights into North Hanover Street and straight on down past the junction with Cathedral Street back to George Square.

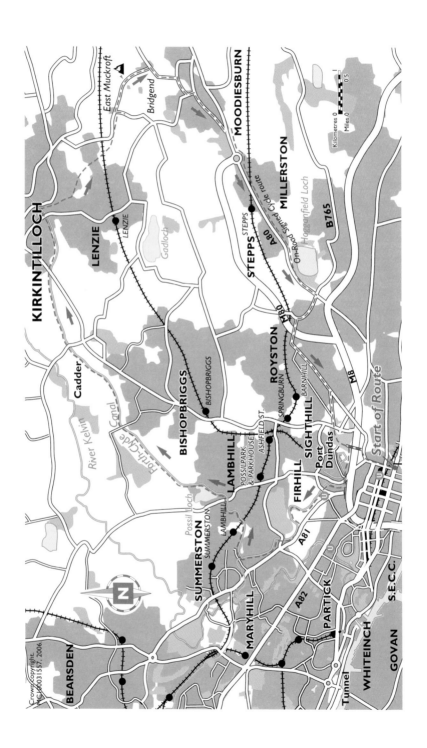

KIRKINTILLOCH

East Muckroft

Bridgend

MOODIESBURN

LENZIE

Lenzie

Gadloch

MILLERSTON

On-Road Signed Cycle route

Hogganfield Loch

STEPPS

Steps

A80

B765

Cadder

Canal

River Kelvin

Forth-Clyde

ROYSTON

BISHOPBRIGGS

Bishopbriggs

SPRINGBURN

BARNHILL

M80

Possil Loch

LAMBHILL

POSSILPARK
& PARKHOUSE

ASHFIELD ST.

SIGHTHILL

Port
Dundas

M8

Start of Route

SUMMERSTON

Summerston

Lambhill

FIRHILL

A81

MARYHILL

A82

PARTICK

S.E.C.C.

Tunnel

WHITEINCH

GOVAN

BEARSDEN

Kilometres 0

Miles 0

0.5

GLASGOW CITY CENTRE TO KIRKINTILLOCH

From George Square to Stockingfield junction on the Forth and Clyde Canal at Maryhill, this route retraces that taken at the end of Route 4. Head north up Hanover Street and on to Baird Street, then quickly turn left into Kyle Street. Carry on across the footbridge which spans the M8 into Sighthill Park and turn along the path to the left. This path finishes at Craighall Road, at which point carry straight on up this road for 400m. Take care here, for this road is often busy. Join the tow-path of the Glasgow branch of the Forth and Clyde Canal at the top of the hill and continue for 3.4 km to the junction of the main canal at Stockingfield.

On reaching Stockingfield junction, the route reverts to the eastern tow-path of the main canal. To get on to the eastern tow-path the traveller must go down the ramp on to Lochburn Road, turn right under the canal bridge, and staying on the same side of the road carry on back up the ramp to the canal tow-path on the other side of the canal.

After 1.5 km or so, the canal passes under Balmore Road Bridge and enters the district of High Possil, passing close to Possil Loch, a large area of marsh that is a Scottish Wildlife Trust Reserve, where huge stocks of wildfowl can be seen. Carry on for 3 km to Balmouldie Road, Bishopbriggs, where you will find Bishopbriggs Sports Centre (which also has a swimming pool).

Another 1.5 km further on is Cadder Church, followed by The Stables at Glasgow Road Bridge (both places are mentioned in Route 2). Then it is only just over 1.5 km further to Kirkintilloch, where the route leaves the canal tow-path.

The tow path comes up to street level at Townhead. Here turn right and follow the road for

INFORMATION

Distance: 40 km (25 miles), circular route.

Map: OS Landranger, sheet 64.

Start and finish: George Square, Glasgow.

Terrain: Generally flat but its length might prove daunting to the unfit or inexperienced cyclist.

Refreshments: Various places in Glasgow. Lock 27, Forth and Clyde Canal, north of Anniesland Cross. Bishopbriggs Sports Centre. The Stables Restaurant and Bar, Glasgow Road Bridge, near Kirkintilloch. Various places in Kirkintilloch. Hogganfield Loch (cafeteria in boathouse).

City Chambers, George Square.

Townhead, Kirkintilloch.

a few hundred metres to the road junction, where there is a set of traffic signals. Go straight on into Industry Street, where an obelisk commemorating James Dalrymple, a Kirkintilloch magistrate, is reached, and immediately beyond this there is a path which enters Woodhead Park. Follow this path through Woodhead Park and then turn right into Parkview Avenue, following it down to the junction with Lenzie Road. Turn left here and almost immediately on the left is the clearly defined footpath following the line of the Monklands and Kirkintilloch railway. The railway once linked the Monklands coalfield with the Forth and Clyde Canal, enabling coal to be taken by barge to Edinburgh.

The 6.4 km to Moodiesburn is no hardship, as it follows the picturesque Bothlin Burn meandering south-east, until the outskirts of Moodiesburn itself are reached. However, a little explanation is necessary at this point. After cycling on the railway path for 800m or so, a crossing of Garngaber Avenue has to be made. Care should be taken here, for although this is a fairly narrow road, cars using it tend to travel quite fast. The path continues on the other side of this road, and for the first 100m or so can be quite muddy. After about another 800m the path narrows and remains like this for about 400m. Here also the path runs right next to a post and wire fence, and there are steps at two points here. As these slight obstacles may make cycling difficult, it may be wise to dismount and walk along this short stretch. The route then comes out on to a minor road, where the railway path recommences on the other side. However, there are several gates along this next stretch of path which are kept locked at all times to prevent animals straying. Although there is access for pedestrians, cyclists have to lift their bikes over these gates. There is no reason why cyclists cannot use this path. If it is used, then in just over 1.5 km it joins Gartferry Road.

Here, however, is an alternative to the use of this path. On joining the minor road, turn left and follow it up the short distance to a T-junction. Here turn right and follow this minor road for 800m to the next road junction. Turn right again and within another 800m Gartferry Road is reached.

At Gartferry Road the route joins the Cumbernauld to Glasgow Cycle Route. This route, although on-road for much of the distance into Glasgow, should present the cyclist with no problems, for most of it is on designated cycle lanes. Just follow this well-signposted route all the way back to Glasgow.

Turn right on to Gartferry Road and follow the route through Cryston and Muirhead and on to the shared footpath for pedestrians and cyclists along the A80 Cumbernauld Road. Continue on to the segregated on-road cycle lane through Stepps past Hogganfield Loch, where refreshments can be had. Turn right into Provanmill Road, then left into Royston Road, using a combination of shared footpath and on-road cycle lane. Turn right into Glenconner Park and then right again into Garnock Street and on to Charles Street, at the end of which take the footbridge over Springburn Road and down the cycle path to Pinkston Road. Turn left down the short cycle path, then right into Sighthill Park and left over the M8 by Kyle Street footbridge, to where this cycle route officially ends.

At Kyle Street turn right into Baird Street, then straight on at the traffic lights into North Hanover Street and straight on down past the junction with Cathedral Street and back into George Square.

Cycles in central Glasgow.

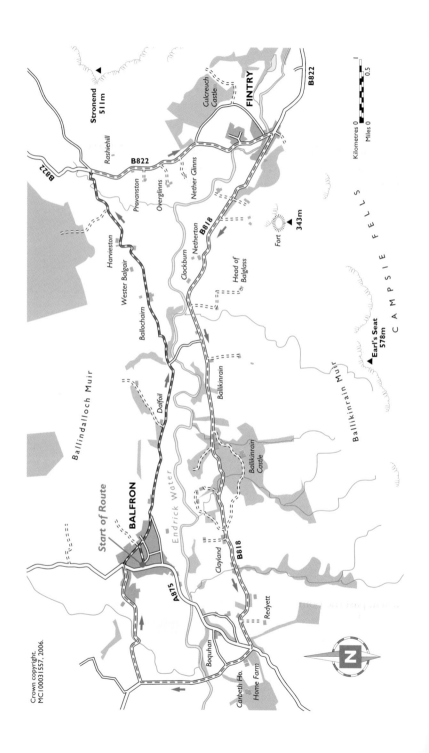

Crown copyright.
MCI 00031557. 2006.

Stronend
511m

Rashiehill

B822

B822

Provanston

Overglinns

Nether Glinns

Culcreuch
Castle

FINTRY

Harvieston

Wester Balgair

Clockburn

Netherton

B818

Fort

343m

Head of
Balglass

Ballochairn

Dalfoil

Ballikinrain

Ballikinrain Muir

Ballindalloch Muir

Start of Route

BALFRON

A875

Clayland

B818

Redyett

Boquhan

Carbeth Ho.

Home Farm

Ballikinrain
Castle

Earl's Seat
578m

C A M P S I E   F E L L S

Kilometres 0
Miles 0
0.5

BALFRON TO FINTRY

The attractive village of Balfron tends to be a dormitory village for people working in Stirling and Glasgow. Its name, according to the *Statistical Account*, is derived from the Gaelic *Bail'a-bhroin*, which means 'village of mourning'. The reason for this mourning is not known. Throughout the centuries village life was dominated by agriculture, but when Ballindalloch Cotton Works was built in 1789, the village saw an influx of many people from surrounding areas coming to work there.

In the middle of the nineteenth century, when the pipeline from Loch Katrine to Glasgow was being laid, the village saw another influx of people. This time they were large gangs of predominantly Irish navvies. According to local folklore, one night a serious incident almost took place which has been known as the Battle of Balfron. This was when two large rival factions of navvies, after a bout of serious drinking, faced up to each other with the intention of settling their differences in a violent manner, but before a blow was struck a message was sent to Stirling Castle and a detachment of troops was despatched to break up the mob. If this story is true, then all I can say is that the opposing armies must have stood looking at each other for a long, long time.

The route from the car park begins by heading north to the top of the town, past the point where Main Street becomes Buchanan Street and on past the junction with Station Road. Soon after Station Road

Balfron Church.

Spectacular views of the
Campsie Fells.

has been passed, turn right into Spoker's Loan
and continue through the junction with Cotton
Street into Roman Road. Take Roman Road
through the remainder of the village and out into
the countryside, where it follows close to the bank
of the Endrick Water, as it gurgles and tumbles
from its source in the Fintry Hills en route towards Loch Lomond. From this road the view to
the south over the Campsie Fells is breathtaking
—from Dumgoyne in the west to Meikle Bin and
beyond in the east. The colours of these hills seem
to be constantly changing as the sunlight rises and
falls over them. Many of the names of the peaks
reflect the presence of the area's leading family,
the Grahams, such as Graham's Cairn, Earl's Seat
and Little Earl.

After some 4 km a road junction is reached. Here
carry straight on, unless you wish to shorten the
bike ride substantially (if so turn right). From here,
over the next 2.4 km, the road begins to climb
slowly, and then plateaus out for the next 1.6 km,
to where it reaches the junction with the B822
Kippen Road. Here turn right and carry on for
the next 2.4 km into the village of Fintry.

The countryside around Fintry is gently hilly with fine grazing land. The plentiful sheep give the area a calm and peaceful aspect, contrasting with the rugged backdrop of the surrounding Campsie Fells. Not surprisingly, its name, which is of Gaelic origin, signifies 'fair land'.

Culcreuch Castle, on the edge of the village, was built in the fifteenth century and was the ancestral home of the clan Galbraith. However, most of the land around this area belonged to the powerful and ancient family of Grahams. In the seventeenth century it belonged to James Graham, the first Marquis of Montrose, who conducted a successful campaign throughout Scotland against the Covenanters. The castle, although it did not belong to the Grahams, was taken over by a Covenanter army as it marched south from Dundee in an attempt to engage Montrose's army and prevent his force from reaching England. On 14 August 1645 the Covenanters did meet Montrose at the Battle of Kilsyth, with terrible consequences for the Covenanters. Later the castle was taken over by the Napier family, then it was sold to Alexander Spiers, who went on to develop the cotton industry and establish the village of Fintry much as it is today. Culcreuch Castle is now a hotel, with part of its grounds turned into a country park.

Cyclist at Fintry.

At the junction of the B811 turn right and follow the B818 back in a westerly direction. The route along the B818 continues for 9.7 km until it reaches the junction with the A875. At this point carry straight on through this junction to the minor road signposted for Balfron Station. After almost 2.4 km another road junction is reached. Here turn right and follow this road the remaining 2.4 km into Balfron, joining Station Road. Turn right into Buchanan Street and then on into Main Street and back to the car park.

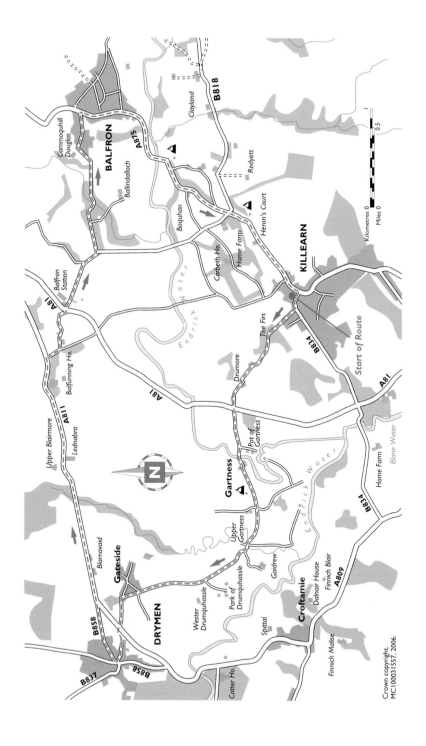

KILLEARN TO BALFRON VIA DRYMEN

his very picturesque route starts at the public car park at the junction of the A875 and Station Road in Killearn.

The village of Killearn lies almost precisely on the Highland Line. It is 9m above sea level, and on a clear day, summer or winter, the views over Loch Lomond and the mountains around it are superb. This cycle route, as it descends to Drymen and then climbs slowly back to Killearn, must be one of the most beautiful routes to be found anywhere in the surrounding country.

Begin down Station Road, heading downhill all the way for about 300m, and then turn right into Gartness Road. After 2.4 km this road crosses the A81, which can be very busy, so take care. Once on the other side, the route soon merges with the West Highland Way, which has by this time joined the road, just before the small village of Gartness, and continues all the way to Drymen.

At Gartness, the Endrick Water once again passes under our route, and it is only a short distance from this spot that the Pot of Gartness is found. At this famous beauty spot the Endrick falls over

INFORMATION

Distance: 18.5 km (11.5 miles), circular route.

Map: OS Landranger, sheet 57.

Start and finish: Public car park, Killearn.

Terrain: Generally undulating until the last 3.2 km (2 miles), when a series of steeper gradients is encountered.

Refreshments: Various places in Killearn, Drymen and Balfron.

Old inn at Killearn.

a rock which spans the river into a deep pool at the bottom. Often salmon and trout can be seen forcing their way up through the torrent of water to the spawning grounds further upstream.

John Napier of Merchiston, inventor of logarithms, is said to have been born at Gartness in 1550 and lived there at various stages throughout his life, including the time around 1614 when he was perfecting his mathematical system.

Dappled light through the trees.

After crossing the bridge over the Endrick Water, the road starts to climb. This short sharp uphill stretch lasts for about 300m, and is quite steep in some places. This is followed by a short undulating stretch before the road once again starts to wind uphill; this time it climbs for about a further 400m until it reaches the highest point of this road, then finally drops down through Gateside and on to the junction with the A811 Dumbarton to Stirling Road.

To cycle into Drymen from here, just turn right and follow the A811 for about 400m to where it merges with the B858. Here double back along this road for a further 400m into Drymen. However, a quicker way is to dismount, cross over the road and take the pedestrian ramp up, a hundred metres or so, to where it joins the Gartness Road once again, which quickly winds down to the centre of Drymen.

The small, but attractive, village of Drymen is a busy place throughout the year, particularly at weekends and holidays, for it is one of the most popular destinations for Glaswegians and others out on an afternoon drive. The village itself (whose name is of Celtic origin, and means ridge or knoll, describing the physical features of the land around the district) is very old, with records of a church being in existence as far back as 1248. Throughout its long history the village has been

Taking a welcome break along the route.

home to those people who worked the lands belonging to the Duke of Montrose, who was the landowner of most of this district.

Once ready to leave Drymen, join the B858 in the direction of Stirling for 400m to where this road merges with the A818, and turn left along it. Carry on for 3.2 km to a minor road on the right, which is signposted to Balfron, and take this road. After about 150m turn left, which is still the Balfron Road, and continue to the junction of the A81. Cross over the A81 into the minor road opposite, called Indies Road. This is Balfron Station, which used to be on the now-disused Caledonian Railway's Glasgow to Stirling line. Within this small cluster of houses the theme would seem decidedly nineteenth-century colonial, for as well as Indies Road there is an Indian Cottage and an Indiesdorp—*dorp* being the Afrikaans word for a group of houses.

Once past this remnant of the British Raj, continue along the road for a little over 1.6 km to the next junction. Here turn left and follow this road, which becomes Station Road, into Balfron.

At the traffic lights turn right on to the A875 and after going through the village the route continues on this road for a further 3.2 km back to Killearn. This part of the route is uphill all the way, with some fairly steep stretches along its length.

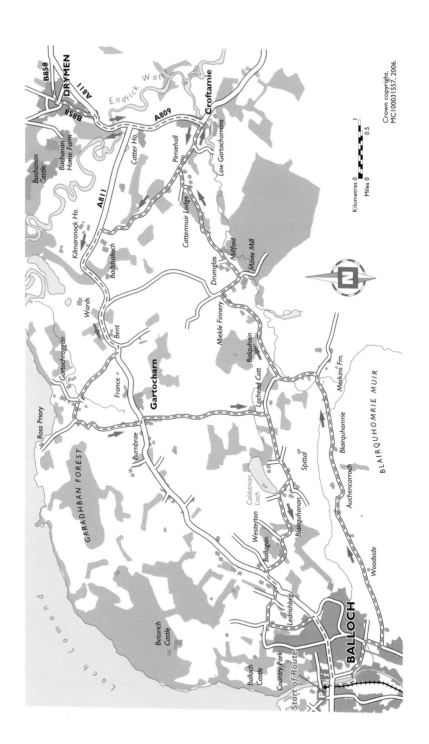

BALLOCH TO DRYMEN

The community at Balloch has developed in modern times through tourism. The first pleasure steamer service on Loch Lomond, the *Marion*, was started in 1818, and there have been pleasure steamers plying up and down the loch ever since. The railway arrived here in 1850, which increased the area's appeal, particularly to day-trippers from Glasgow.

This route starts in Balloch at the car park opposite the Railway Station. From here follow the cycle route signposted in the direction of Dumbarton along the west bank of the River Leven. After 800m, turn left across a bridge over the river, and after a short distance turn right on to the A813. Carry on along this road for 800m and turn left into Auchencarroch Road. The road climbs fairly consistently for the next 3.2 km through Blairquhomrie Muir, with its heather-clad and mossy slopes. As there are no particularly steep inclines to contend with along this stretch, and as the prevailing wind is at the cyclist's back, no real problems should be encountered here. Once at the top of this hill, the route stays relatively flat until the descent into Balloch, almost at the end of the journey. This road is a pleasant, minor country road with little traffic to bother about. However

INFORMATION

Distance: 30 km (18 miles), circular route.

Map: OS Landranger, sheets 56, 63 and 64.

Start and finish: Balloch Railway Station. For those arriving by car there is a car park opposite the station.

Terrain: Generally undulating.

Refreshments: Various places in Balloch, Gartocharn, Croftamie and Drymen.

Loch Lomond..

care must be taken, for at various points along the way some double bends have to be negotiated.

After cycling on this road for about 5 km you reach a 4-way junction. Here turn left, following the sign for Croftamie, and travel past Caldarvan Station, which reminds us that there was once a railway in these parts. After 800m a T-junction is reached. Still following the signs for Croftamie, turn right. This pleasant road continues for another 1.6 km to where another T-junction is reached. Following the sign for Croftamie, turn right along this road past Mavie Mill and on to the junction at Pirniehall. Here turn right and follow the road to Croftamie. At Croftamie join the A809 through the village, taking great care at the junction of the A811 a little over 1.6 km further on. Once on the A811 the route passes over the fine 5-spanned stone bridge crossing the Endrick Water. It is then but a short distance to the B858, which is the road into Drymen.

At this point in the journey, the cyclist has the opportunity, if so desired, of continuing onward using the cycle route to Killin, which from the village of Drymen continues northward using the extensive forestry tracks through the Garadhban Forest and the Queen Elizabeth Forest, passing, en route, Aberfoyle and Callander. The Killin cycle route is intended to link into the Glasgow to Loch Lomond cycle route. It is also part of the Sustrans Inverness to Dover route.

For the purposes of this route, however, after Drymen has been explored or a break has been taken, return to the junction at Pirniehall by the same route in reverse. From this junction, this time take the right fork on to the minor road signposted for Gartocharn. This road falls steadily to the junction of the A811, and at this point you turn left along this road. Although this A-class road can be busy, it should not cause concern for cyclists. However, you should take care when cycling here. The route uses this road for about 3 km before turning right at the junction signposting a campsite. This is a loop road, which, although slightly longer, takes the cyclist to Gartocharn by a more peaceful and picturesque route. However, the road is quite bumpy in places. It passes close to Ross Priory, once owned by the powerful Buchanan family. It has now been taken over by the University of Strathclyde as a sports and social club. On the second half of this loop, as the road rises slightly towards Gartocharn, there are splendid views of the loch and the mountains, which so dramatically separate the Highlands from Central Scotland. While gazing at this remarkable sight it is not hard to imagine the terrain being carved out by melting glaciers at the end of the Ice Age.

On reaching Gartocharn, turn left along the A811 for about 200m and turn right into School Road. This climbs steadily for 800m, then flattens out. After you have been on this road for 2.4 km a T-junction is reached. Here turn right and follow the sign for Balloch. After 1.5 km or so, this road drops fairly steeply downhill. Take care not to go too fast down this hill, for there are two very tight double bends to negotiate before the road once again joins the A811. Here turn left and follow this main road once again for about 800m, and then turn right into Drymen Road and carry on along this road, now in Balloch, for about 800m back to the car park opposite the railway station.

Boats on the River Leven at Balloch.

Well worth a visit, at this point, is Balloch Castle and Country Park, where more magnificent views of the south end of Loch Lomond can be seen. The castle was built in 1808 for John Buchanan of Ardoch. The estate was bought by Glasgow Corporation in 1915. The grounds were turned into a public park, which it remained until 1981, when it became a Country Park, with the castle becoming its visitors' centre.

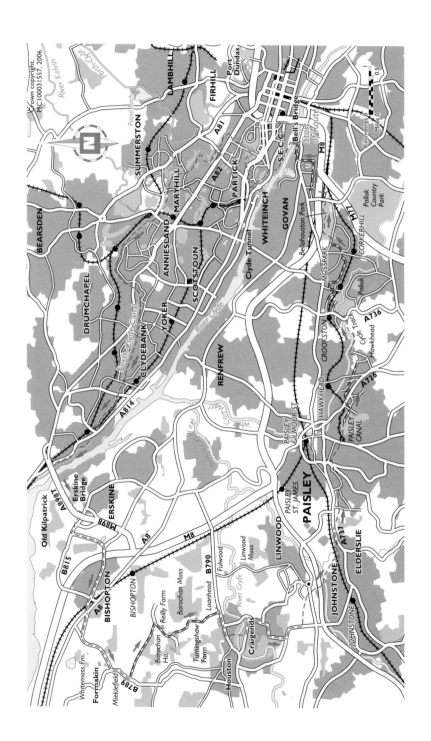

BELL'S BRIDGE, GLASGOW, TO ERSKINE BRIDGE

Follow this clearly signposted, designated cycleway, as route 4, for just over 1 km to Old Dumbarton Road, turn right on to it and follow this road past its junction with Benalder Street. Here turn left into Bunhouse Road, passing the Museum of Transport on the right. This is a designated cycle route, so it is clearly defined.

At the end of this cycle route, cross Argyle Street by means of the Toucan Crossing and continue into the western end of Kelvingrove Park. On the right you will see the Kelvingrove Museum and Art Gallery, and as you will have gathered there is plenty to see in this area. Both buildings have cycle parking, so it is easy to stop here.

After entering the park, take the path to the left and continue over the River Kelvin. On the other side, carry on along the high path (this means negotiating a fairly steep hill for a short distance) and cycle on to its end at Kelvin Way. Cross the road and re-enter the park on the other side and soon you will go over the river again by the first of the many fine Victorian bridges that you will find along this route. From here take the path on the left by the east bank of the river and head downhill. After 300m or so, turn left on to a wooden slatted walkway which makes its way under the bridge at Gibson Street and continues along the riverside. Now the route is easy: just keep on the path running alongside the river. Once you have passed underneath the bridge at Great Western Road, you will find it hard to remember that you are still within a major city, it feels as though you are deep in the countryside. After some 350m the river is crossed once again. As you continue heading west, the ruins of the North Woodside flint mill are

INFORMATION

Distance: 50 km (31 miles), circular route.

Map: OS Landranger, sheet 64.

Start and finish: Bell's Bridge. Just take the train to Exhibition Centre and follow the signed pedestrian/cycle route to the SECC. Or if coming by car, use the Scottish Exhibition and Conference Centre car park, Glasgow.

Terrain: Generally fairly flat, but its distance might be daunting for the unfit or inexperienced cyclist.

Refreshments: Various places en route.

Kelvingrove Museum and Art Gallery.

One of the fine Victorian bridges over the Kelvin.

passed on the left. The mill was built in 1846, on the site of an old grain mill, to grind flints for pottery glazes. It closed during the 1960s, but the ruins, including a kiln, weir and mill lade, have been preserved. Carry on for a short distance and under another of the many beautiful bridges en route, this time by means of a short tunnel. At the other side there is a footbridge which gives access to the Botanic Gardens, which are well worth a visit. One of the highlights here is the Kibble Palace, a spectacular glasshouse which houses many species of tropical plants. Originally built in 1873, it has recently been renovated by the City Council. Continue west to the Ha'penny Bridge, cross this to the other side of the river once more and enter the Arboretum. Cycle through this delightful area, opened in 1975, which holds many plants from North America. Cross the river yet again, turn left and follow the path uphill and on to the junction with Kelvindale Road; after crossing this, continue on the path on the other side. After almost a kilometre, the aqueduct which carries the Forth and Clyde Canal is reached. At this point take the path on the right, which heads steeply uphill, to the tow-path and cycle west (in the opposite direction to that described in latter half of chapter 4) to Clydebank, here keeping to the tow-path.

Clydebank is the birthplace of three of the four Queens of the Cunard Line. These great ships, the *Queen Mary*, *Queen Elizabeth* and *Queen Elizabeth II*, were constructed at the famous John Brown's shipyard in the centre of Clydebank. Clydebank was built in the latter part of the nineteenth century, around the shipyards which were springing up on that part of the Clyde. Clydebank suffered very badly during the Second World War. Between 13 and 14 March 1941, German bombers dropped hundreds of tons of bombs on the town, killing 534 people and injuring 790 more, with 4,300 houses destroyed and another 7,700 badly damaged. In all only 8 houses in the town were left standing intact.

Continue on the tow-path all the way to Old Kilpatrick, where the Erskine Bridge spans the River Clyde. Here, just before the canal flows under this gigantic road bridge, leave the tow-path, cross the canal bridge and turn left on to the A814. Carry on along this road, under Erskine Bridge, for almost 800m to a junction on the right which is signposted for Glasgow. Go along Station Road and head uphill past Kilpatrick Railway Station and carry on until you have almost reached the bridge under the A82. Here turn left into Mountpleasant Drive, which winds round to a narrow road bridge. At the other side of this bridge, turn right and follow the path around the edge of a sports field to where there is a sign pointing the way across the Erskine Bridge for cyclists. It is possible to cycle on either side of the bridge, north or south.

The crossing of this 2.4 km-long cable-stayed box-girder bridge, the deck of which is 55m above the river, can be an exhilarating experience. However, I can assure the reader it is quite safe. Stop for a while at the centre of the main span for a look at the view back over the entire distance you have covered on this route thus far.

On the south side of the bridge the cycle path heads down to join a roundabout. On the west side of this roundabout it joins the B815 and the continuation of the route. Here it would be best to dismount and walk to the B815, thus avoiding this busy roundabout. Here is also the entrance to Erskine Hospital, which looks after those injured while serving in the armed forces.

After joining the B815, carry on for just over 800m, through another roundabout, to Erskine Parish Church. Opposite this beautiful old building there is Drumcross Road, which heads south. Take this road for 1.2 km to the junction with Old Greenock Road. Here turn right and follow this road all the way through the village of Bishopton. At the signalised junction with Ferry Road and Old Greenock Road, carry straight on into Parton Place. There is a no-entry for vehicles sign here, but the two-way street continues on the other side of the junction. At the end of this road turn right on to the A8, only to leave it again immediately by turning left on to the minor road, which is, in fact, still Old Greenock Road and which is signposted for Houston and Johnstone. After about 1.5 km a three-way junction is reached. Head left on to the road which has a sign saying it is unsuitable for heavy vehicles. This winds downhill towards the Formakin Estate. On this road one gets wide views over Renfrewshire. At the bottom of the hill is Formakin Estate, which was built between 1902 and 1913 for the rich Paisley stockbroker John Augustus Holms.

A short distance after passing Formakin, the route joins the B789. Turn left and continue for 800m or so to the junction with a minor road. Turn left on to this very quiet 3m-wide unclassified road. The first section of this road runs next to the southern boundary fence of the former Royal Ordnance factory, but then it turns into open country, on past Turningshaw Farm, to the junction of the B790. Here turn right along this road for 800m to the beginning of the town of Houston, where the 40 mile an hour sign indicates where you should turn left into Ardgryffe Crescent. Where this road runs parallel to the Gryffe Water you will see a bridge over the river on the left. Leave the road, cross this bridge and take the path on the right up a slight incline for 200m or so, to where a pathway connects to Crawford Road. Once on Crawford Road, go through this housing estate to the junction of Magnus Road and turn left on to it. Continue along this road, which changes its name to Fulton Drive. At the end of Fulton Drive, turn left into Barochan Road, continue for a short distance to the next junction and turn right, still keeping on Barochan Road. After another 500m turn right on to the Irvine to Glasgow

Old mill by the Cart.

cycle route NCN 7. Once down the short ramp, turn left following the signs for Paisley and Glasgow. Follow this cycleway through Elderslie, the birthplace of Sir William Wallace (1274-1305), and then on to Paisley.

Paisley is an ancient town, founded about 560 by Mirin, a missionary Irish monk, who built a church on the east bank of the Cart. In 1163 Walter Fitzalan founded Paisley Abbey with Cistercian monks brought from Shropshire. The abbey was damaged by fire, first by Edward I's army in 1307, and then again in 1498. However, undaunted, the monks had it rebuilt each time.

In the eighteenth century Paisley became famous for two industries: weaving and thread-making. Paisley has many fine Victorian buildings, which include the Town Hall and the Observatory, gifted by the Coates family to the town in 1882, which has been recording astronomical and meteorological information ever since. Continue along the cycle route to Glasgow, where the route ends at the south side of Bell's Bridge.

There is a set of extremely informative, easy-to-use, leaflets for both the Glasgow to Loch Lomond cycle route and the Clyde Coast cycle routes (of which Glasgow to Paisley and Paisley to Greenock are part). This series of leaflets is available at all tourist information centres.

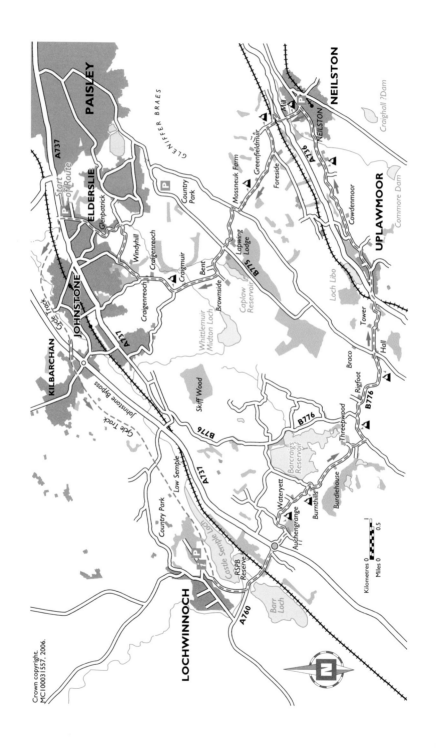

Crown copyright.
MC100031557, 2006.

ELDERSLIE TO LOCHWINNOCH
VIA UPLAWMOOR

Elderslie (previously known as Ellersly), which was once a village on its own, now forms part of the Paisley/Johnstone conurbation. It is, however, a very historic place, with evidence of a settlement going back to the Bronze Age about 2,300 years ago.

The best-known family to have lived in the area were the Wallaces of Ellersly. Their castle would have been situated where the Wallace monument stands today. The first member of the Wallace family to settle in Scotland was Richard de Wals, a Norman knight who came north with King David I in 1124 and settled in Ayrshire. It was his son, Sir Malcolm Wallace, who built the castle at Elderslie. He married Margaret Craufurd, the daughter of the Sheriff of Ayr, and there in 1270 his son William was born. William Wallace was the great hero who did so much for Scotland in the War of Independence, until his horrific death at the hands of the English in 1305. He was caught and taken to London, where at a mock trial he was sentenced to death, then barbarously executed by being hung, drawn and quartered and his head nailed to London Bridge.

In more modern times Elderslie has been famous for its carpets, for here was Stoddard's carpet factory, world famous for the production of high-quality carpets for almost a century.

The route starts at the car park in Stoddart Square opposite the Public Library. Turn right out of the car park and then turn right again into Glenpatrick Road. Immediately ahead is the controlled junction at Main Street. Cross this into Canal Street, at the bottom of which the Glasgow to Irvine/Ardrossan cycleway continues along the disused railway towards Johnstone. However, in just over

INFORMATION

Distance: 24.1 km (15 miles), circular route.

Map: OS Landranger, sheets 63 and 64.

Start and finish: Stoddart Square car park, Elderslie. Alternatively, Elderslie can be reached by train from Glasgow Central Station.

Terrain: The first part of this route is generally fairly flat, but after Lochwinnoch there are stretches of fairly steep hills, some quite lengthy, particularly between Neilston and Elderslie. If you do not wish to over-exert yourself, then turn at Lochwinnoch and return via the cycle route.

Refreshments: Various places in Elderslie, Lochwinnoch and Uplawmoor.

800m the cycleway comes to the Johnstone bypass, where a footbridge spans this road. This is the junction of two cycle tracks: the one crossing the footbridge is to Greenock via Kilmacolm, and the other, which we take, continues along the east side of the bypass and goes by way of Johnstone to Irvine and Seamill.

Johnstone has been marked on maps for many hundreds of years. The Old Brig at Johnstone was the only place to cross the Black Cart Water between here and the River Clyde some miles to the north, so Johnstone would have been on the road through Renfrewshire from Paisley to Ardrossan. Johnstone or Ihonstoun, which just means 'John's settlement', was formally designed and built as a town in 1782 to house the families of the workers in the pits and quarries around the area. There was also a tradition of linen thread spinning in this area.

Physically joined to Johnstone to the south-west is Kilbarchan, which the route bisects. The latter was an eighteenth-century weaving village with characteristic 2-storey cottages, which were both home and weaving shop. One of these cottages has now been taken over by the National Trust for

Lochwinnoch.

Scotland and completely restored to show how it would have looked in the eighteenth century. Its loom is still in working order, and weaving demonstrations are given at certain times.

For the next 6.4 km along this well-defined cycleway, the route is through pleasant wooded countryside until it reaches Lochwinnoch, the last 3.2 km being along the banks of Castle Semple Loch.

Lochwinnoch, meaning 'Saint Winnoc's loch', is a point from where visitors can gain access to Muirshiel Country Park, the first Regional Park created in the country. This fine park opens a 363 sq. km area of countryside to the public all the way from Lochwinnoch to Cloch Point on the Clyde coast, with nature

The entrance to Muirshiel Park.

trails, bird sanctuaries, moorland, rivers, lochs and woodland. Most of this land is still used for farming, so be vigilant: keep to the prescribed paths, keep control of your dogs, and don't start fires. Castle Semple water park is also part of the regional park area, offering facilities for all sorts of water sports. The third area of interest is the Royal Society for the Protection of Birds' Nature Centre, with an observation tower, nature trails and bird-watching hides. These facilities are all well signposted from Lochwinnoch, which is itself an attractive rural village with a small agricultural museum. It's worth noting, however, that the entrance to Muirshiel Park is some 6 km from Lochwinnoch. This is reached by way of the B786 Bridge of Weir Road and from there on to the unclassified road to Muirshiel.

At Lochwinnoch the route leaves the cycleway at Church Street by carrying straight on where the cycle route turns right. Carry on along Church Street over the River Calder and turn left on to

Cyclists at Lochwinnoch.

the new cycle path which goes on all the way to Lochwinnoch Station, passing the Nature Centre en route. From the station, carry on along the A760 which can be quite busy, so take care, for 1 km to the roundabout, which forms the junction with the A737. Here continue straight on, once around the roundabout, to the unclassified road which is signed Auchengrange Hill leading to Belltrees Road. This road climbs uphill fairly steeply for 400m to the junction with Belltrees Road. Here turn left, and continue along this road after first stopping to take in the view of the valley below. Carry on a further 400m to where another junction is reached. A right turn should be made here. This quiet minor road continues uphill at various gradients, some of which are fairly steep, followed by a short but steep descent down to yet another junction, which is next to the wall of Barcraigs Reservoir, and turn right again. Cycle uphill again past Newmills Cottage, after which it gets steeper for a short distance. On the way up this hill there is a good view over the Barcraigs Reservoir. This is a very picturesque part of the route, with many fine views over Kirkleegreen and Cuffhill Reservoirs and over to Cuff Hill and Lochlands

A reed-bed near the route.

Hill beyond. Thereafter the road drops downhill, turning left at the next two junctions encountered. Carry on now for 800m to the junction with the B776, where a right turn is made towards Uplaw-moor. Once again climb uphill for 800m and then head down to the junction with the B775, where a fine old baronial hall can be seen on the right. Go straight on at this junction to where this road meets the A736. Here turn left and join this busy road for 200m or so before turning right into the village of Uplawmoor. Carry on through this picturesque village and take the road signposted for Neilston 4 km ahead. At Neilston Main Street, turn left into Holehouse Brae and carry on down-hill to the A736 once again. Here turn left and immediately right on to the minor road which leads on over the Lochliboside Hills to Johnstone. This is where the road really starts to climb steeply, and it does so for about 1.5 km, passing en route a T-junction, at which the road to the left should be taken. At the top of the hill, pause for a look at the view over towards Paisley and on as far as Glasgow. Here turn right at the white house and follow the road along to Mossneuk Farm. Here turn right. Then, after only 200m, turn left and continue to the B775. Cross this T-junction and continue along this minor road, which descends for most of the way, for 4 km, following signs for Johnstone. Take care on this stretch, for there are two double bends to negotiate.

On entering the upper part of Johnstone, this road becomes Auchenlodment Road. Continue along this road for about 1.6 km to the junction with Kings Road, which veers off to the right (just before the fire station). Take Kings Road a short distance, then turn right into Cemetery Road. After passing the cemetery, this road changes its name to Abbey Road. Continue for 400m to a T-junction and turn left into Glenpatrick Road. Carry on almost to the end of this road, at which point turn right into Stoddart Square, where the route began.

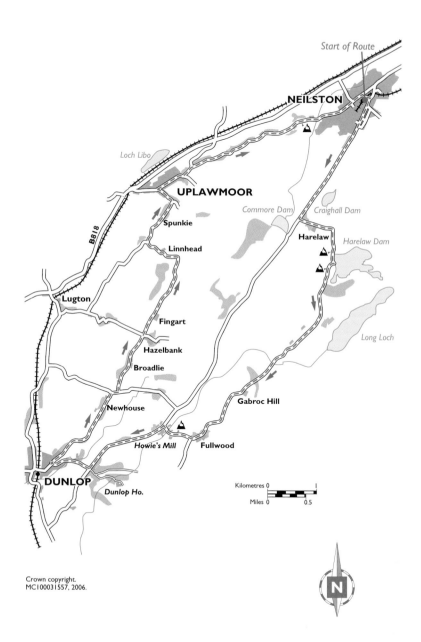

Start of Route

NEILSTON

Loch Libo

UPLAWMOOR

B818

Spunkie

Commore Dam   Craighall Dam

Linnhead

Harelaw   Harelaw Dam

Lugton

Fingart

Long Loch

Hazelbank

Broadlie

Newhouse

Gabroc Hill

Howie's Mill   Fullwood

DUNLOP

Dunlop Ho.

Kilometres 0   1

Miles 0   0.5

N

NEILSTON TO DUNLOP

Neilston was merely a small collection of houses until the Industrial Revolution, although there is evidence of a church in the area since the twelfth century. The village grew rapidly owing to the availability of fresh clean water, being an ideal spot to set up industries such as thread mills, calico printing, dying, bleaching and laundries. However, by the middle of the nineteenth century all but one thread mill had ceased to exist. Today Neilston has become a dormitory town for Paisley and Glasgow and has increased greatly in size. This is due in part to the reopening of the railway in the 1970s.

At Neilston Station car park turn right into Corseton Brae and carry on along this road as it winds uphill, sometimes quite steeply, for 3.2 km. At this point turn left, at a crossroads, along the unclassified road towards Harelaw Dam. Just before the road reaches the dam there is a short but very steep gradient to contend with, and just as the road begins to flatten out, another even steeper section has to be negotiated. However, soon the top is reached, where fine views over

INFORMATION

Distance: 24 km (15 miles), circular route.

Map: OS Landranger, sheet 64.

Start and finish: Neilston Railway Station car park.

Terrain: This route is generally undulating, with two short stretches of very steep hills, gradient about 1 in 5.

Refreshments: Various places in Neilston, Dunlop and Uplawmoor.

Harelaw Dam.

View over to Arran.

Harelaw Dam, the adjacent Long Loch and the surrounding countryside can be had.

After about 1.5 km the road leaves Renfrewshire and enters north Ayrshire, where it continues for an undulating 3.2 km to a junction. On a clear day there are wonderful views over to the Isle of Arran, with a white cap of snow on top of Goat Fell. Turn right down a hill for 800m, past Howie's Mill, to the junction just beyond. Here turn left and follow this road towards Dunlop, turning right at the next road junction, which is opposite Dunlop House.

The route continues on another 800m to a junction. Here turn right and follow this minor road as it gradually climbs uphill for about 1.5 km, at which point it levels out for a short distance before reaching a T-junction. Turn right and follow the road signposted for Uplawmoor, which within a few metres turns left at the next road junction. Follow this fairly flat road straight on through the next junction for 4 km to a T-junction, at which point turn right. On the west side of the road, on a farm called Spunkie, there is a most handsome herd of Highland cattle. As the road enters the village of Uplawmoor, it becomes Tannoch Road and this joins Neilston Road opposite Caldwell Parish Church.

Uplawmoor was first mentioned in a Charter of James, Chancellor of Scotland, in 1294 as the Uplayis, meaning, in this case, a place lying outside Paisley Abbey lands. However, this sleepy little village changed little until this century, relying until then on handloom weaving and agriculture for its population of 200 to make its living. Today this attractive village, which lies almost on the border with Ayrshire, is mainly a residential area for those working in Glasgow or Paisley.

Turn right on to Neilston Road and continue through the village. On the way through, the route passes Uplawmoor Inn, which was said to have been a hideout for smugglers from Ayrshire. This of course was a long time ago, for today it is a pleasant hotel with a beer garden at the rear facing out on to the village green. From this vantage point one can keep an eye on the bikes while partaking of some refreshment and watching the village cricket team play.

At the end of the village, veer left onto the road which is signposted for Neilston. The last 4 km into Neilston is mainly flat until the village is reached and then the road climbs up to join Main Street. Just before the centre of the town turn right into Station Road and back to the station car park.

Jacob's sheep graze by the road.

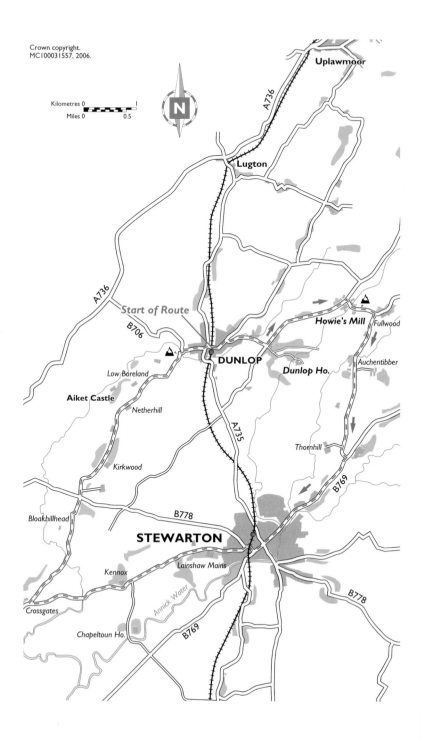

Crown copyright.
MC100031557, 2006.

Kilometres 0 ——————— 1
Miles 0 ———— 0.5

N

Uplawmoor

A736

Lugton

A736

B706

Start of Route

Howie's Mill   Fullwood

DUNLOP

Dunlop Ho.

Auchentibber

Low Boreland

Aiket Castle

Netherhill

A735

Thornhill

Kirkwood

B769

Bloakhillhead

B778

STEWARTON

Kennox

Lainshaw Mains

Annick Water

B778

Crossgates

Chapeltoun Ho.

B769

DUNLOP TO STEWARTON

The village of Dunlop is built on the site of a fort, which would have been constructed by one of the many noble Norman families who were granted lands in this area by King David I in the twelfth century. This mainly agricultural village is famous for a type of cheese which takes its name from the village. Barbara Gilmore, the wife of a local farmer, had to take refuge in Ireland because she was a Covenanter. There she learned of a different process of cheese-making which, on her return home, she developed into the well-known Dunlop cheese.

Dunlop, which has now been declared a conservation area, is a very interesting and picturesque village with its rows of traditional eighteenth-century terraced cottages, the Parish Church built in 1835 and Kirkland House built in 1781, which was once the manse.

This route begins at Dunlop Station car park. Turn right out of the car park on to Newmill Road. Soon a road junction is reached, at which point turn right following the larger of the two roads. After about 800m turn left on to a minor road opposite

INFORMATION

Distance: 20.5 km (12.7 miles), circular route.

Map: OS Landranger, sheets 63 and 64.

Start and finish: Dunlop Railway Station car park.

Terrain: Generally flat with undulating stretches.

Refreshments: Various places in Dunlop and Stewarton.

Kirkland House, Dunlop.

Aitket Castle.

the entrance to Dunlop House, and carry on for 1.5 km to Howie's Mill. Here turn right down by the side of the mill and follow this minor road, as it climbs, to the next junction. Turn right here and carry on, downhill, to the junction with the B769. Follow this road for 2.4 km into Stewarton.

Carry straight on through Main Street in Stewarton to the mini-roundabout and take the B778, signposted for Kilwinning. After a short distance this road passes under a railway bridge, after which turn left on to Kilwinning Road, leaving the B778 at this point. After 1.6 km the road starts to wind uphill for about 400m, and then it levels out briefly before climbing again for another 400m. Turn right 4.8 km from Stewarton at Crossgates Farm and follow this road, also a minor road, back to the junction of the B778, a further 2.4 km. At this junction carry straight on over this road and continue along the minor road on the other side back in the direction of Dunlop. This road winds uphill quite steeply for a short distance and then continues to climb much more gradually for about 800m before levelling off. The road then carries on along the top of an escarpment, which provides an excellent view of the valley below. In this valley is situated Aitket Castle, which was built by Alexander Cunningham in 1479. The original 4-storey tower was added to and altered over the centuries, but sadly it was badly damaged by fire in 1957. Since then the castle has undergone a major restoration by its present owner. However, it is not open to the public.

The road then commences downhill into the village of Dunlop. After crossing the bridge which spans the Glazert Burn, the road climbs up to the junction at Main Street. Turn right here and follow the road up to the centre of the village. Then turn left on to Stewarton Road, quickly right into Newmill Road, over the railway bridge and back to where the route began at Dunlop Station.

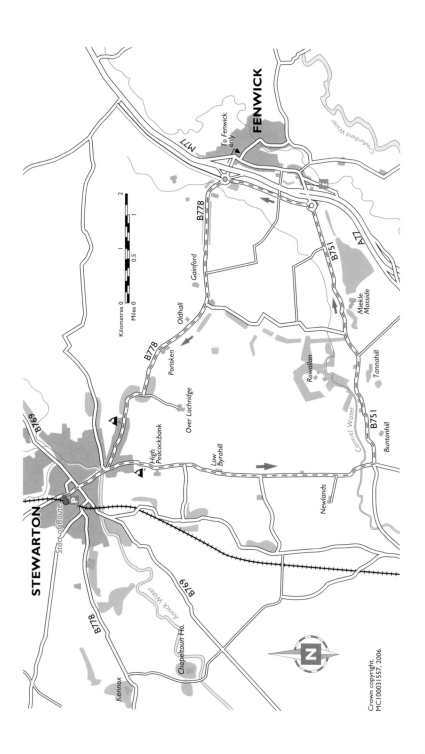

Crown copyright.
MC100031557, 2006.

STEWARTON TO FENWICK

At Stewarton Railway Station car park turn right on to Rigg Street. Take care here, for this is a busy road, and follow it down and through the junction with Main Street into Vennel Street.

This town takes its name from the first High Steward of Scotland, Walter Fitzalan, who was appointed by King David I and who was granted lands in the area. His descendant, also called Walter, married Robert the Bruce's daughter, Marjory. When their son Robert succeeded to the throne in 1377, he was the first of the Stewart dynasty which ruled Scotland for the next three centuries. Stewarton is, however, best known as the Bonnet Toun, and has existed as such since 1650, or at least that is when records of the trade were started, but it is likely that bonnets were made in this area long before then.

On reaching Vennel Street, continue uphill to a junction and carry straight on along the Kilmaurs Road to Kilmarnock Road. Keep on this minor road as it winds uphill for 1.5 km, to where a

INFORMATION

Distance: 14.5 km (9 miles), circular route.

Map: OS Landranger, sheets 64 and 70.

Start and finish: Stewarton Railway Station car park.

Terrain: Generally undulating.

Refreshments: Various places in Stewarton and Fenwick.

Stewarton.

Fenwick Parish Church.

Covenanter's tomb in
Fenwick churchyard.

fine view of the Firth of Clyde, as far south as the
Ailsa Craig, can be seen. This undulating but very
straight road continues for 4.8 km to the junction
of the B751 road to Fenwick.

Turn left, and after about 1.5 km the road
passes Rowallan Castle, which is situated by the
Carmel Water a little to the
north. This imposing castle,
a mix of architecture from
the thirteenth, fifteenth and
sixteenth centuries, was the
birthplace of Robert II's wife,
Elizabeth Mure. It has, fairly
recently, undergone extensive
renovation and is not open
to the public. Continue for
3.2 km to where this B-class
road joins the A77 at a new
roundabout.

Here proceed along the A77
on the cycleway to the next
roundabout, where, if you
want to go into Fenwick you
turn right, and if you want to

Standing stone at Stewarton.

go straight back to Stewarton you turn left, and proceed along the B778. This quiet road slowly climbs for about 3 km to its highest point, where once again, on a clear day, incredible views over the Firth of Clyde and south Ayrshire can be seen. The road then starts its quite steep descent into Stewarton, so take care. After entering the town, the road joins the minor road to Kilmaurs. Turn right at this junction and retrace the route through Vennel Street, on to Rigg Street and back to Stewarton Station.

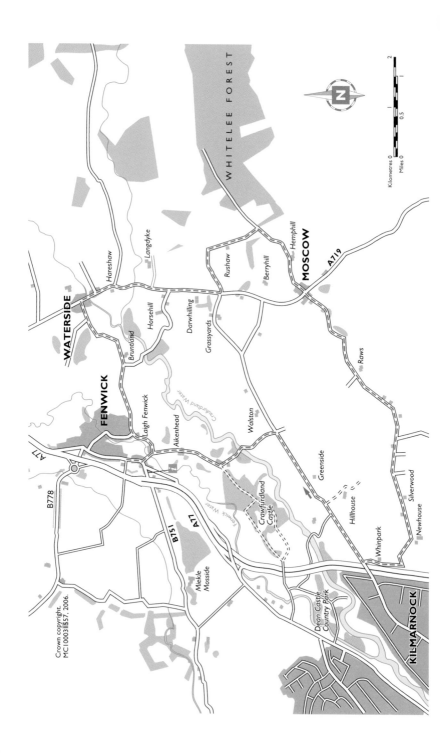

FENWICK TO MOSCOW

Fenwick today is mainly a residential village, but in the eighteenth century handloom weaving was established in Laigh Fenwick, which is the lower part of the town.

There are no public car parks in Fenwick, so the route starts from Main Street, which is the B751, where there are no parking restrictions. Turn into Waterslap, which is signposted for Waterside, and after only about 200m turn left, still following the signs for Waterside. The first 2.4 km of this route are uphill, with the latter part, which is almost the whole way to Waterside, being quite steep. At this very small but picturesque village beside Craufurdland Water, turn right on to the A719, known as the Galston Road, and continue down this undulating road for 2 km. At this point a 4-way junction is to be found. Here turn left and follow this very narrow minor road to the entrance of Raithmuir Farm and turn right. The road surface here is a little bumpy. Carry on to a T-junction, turn right and follow the road downhill to Moscow.

Sadly, the reason for naming this little village after the somewhat larger conurbation in Russia is lost in obscurity. Its original name is thought to have been derived from the word Mosshaugh, meaning a corner of peaty moorland, and why it should have been changed to Moscow can now only be a matter for conjecture. One explanation is that, in the nineteenth century, the name was probably changed as a gimmick because of news being reported about the Napoleonic Wars, and has stuck ever since. To enhance the Russian flavour of the area, the local burn was named the

King's Arms, Fenwick.

Volga. Furthermore the village was visited by the Soviet Prime Minister Alexei Nikolayevich Kosygin during a visit to Scotland in 1965.

The mystery surrounding this little village is not confined to its name, for it is also the scene of one Scotland's most notorious unsolved murders. On 12 March 1884, Mr Robert Rankin, a respected Kilmarnock businessman, was found brutally murdered by strangling in his home in Volga Bank Cottage, Moscow. He had also received many blows to the head and body. Strangely, his assailant had tried to make this brutal attack look like suicide by placing a hammer in the dead man's hand. However, it is hard to understand how the murderer could have expected the police to accept that the victim had struck himself about the head and body with a hammer so often and with such ferocity that he brought about his own death. Although a man was detained the following week on suspicion, no evidence could be found to implicate him and he was subsequently released. To this day, this crime has remained a complete mystery. It caused such a stir in the area that a local Kilmarnock newspaper reported that: 'on Sunday last, Moscow was visited by large numbers of visitors

Volga Bank Cottage, Moscow.

from the town [Kilmarnock], attracted thither by morbid curiosity and the fineness of the weather. The village inn was literally besieged by thirsty travellers, who were admitted in relays until the entire stock of liquor was exhausted'. The reason for this interest was simply that, at this time, there was no serious crime in Kilmarnock, and the act of murder was completely unheard of.

Another point of interest in Moscow is a house (also in Hemphill) which has a stained-glass front door in the design of a Soviet Russian postage stamp depicting the crest of the Federation of Soviet Farmers. This house is currently owned by Mr and Mrs Matt Donald, who don't mind people stopping to have a look at their interesting door.

The route continues over the A719 along the minor road which is, for the next stretch, still undulating. At 10.5 km there is a junction, but the route is straight on following the sign for Kilmarnock. At this point, on a clear day, there is a beautiful view over the Firth of Clyde as far as the Ailsa Craig, and in particular the Isle of Arran shows itself at its splendid best. After another 2.4 km this road begins to run parallel to the A77 for a short distance, but then soon comes to a T-junction. Here turn right at the sign for Waterside, and take this road uphill once again, for another 2.4 km, to the junction with the Fenwick Road. Here turn left into this road, and soon it goes over a beautiful stone bridge which spans Crawfurdland Water. Here this fast-flowing stream has gouged a 91 m deep gorge out of the surrounding landscape. This is close to Crawfurdland Castle (not open to the public), the ancient home of the Crawfurd family, which dates from the fourteenth century, and which still belongs to the family today.

This road now continues, through pleasant, gently rolling, agricultural land, for the remaining 2.4 km back to Fenwick.

Russian postage stamp in stained glass, Moscow.

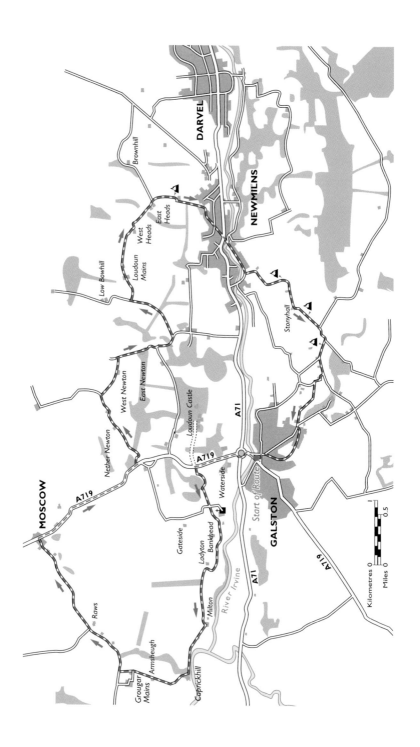

GALSTON TO NEWMILNS VIA MOSCOW

Galston is located 6.4 km east of Kilmarnock. Because the town lies within a fertile valley on the River Irvine, there has been a settlement in Galston for many thousands of years. There was a Roman camp here which served the garrison built on top of Loudoun Hill, a few miles to the east.

Some of the places of interest in the area include Barr Castle, which was built in the fifteenth century and where John Knox preached in 1556, and St Sophia's Church, which is unusually built in the Byzantine style. Perhaps this church's architectural style, and it being given the name of an East European saint, adds some credence to the myth of this area's association with Russia!

The route starts at Wallace Street. Start off in a northerly direction and carry on over the bridge which spans the River Irvine, and within a short distance a major roundabout is reached at the junction of the A71 and A719. I recommend that you dismount here and negotiate this very busy roundabout on foot, using the adjacent footpaths, and on the other side start cycling again along the much quieter A719. After only 800m on this A-class road, turn left on to a very quiet minor road, which is in fact the first junction you meet after passing the roundabout.

Head downhill, following this road past a beautiful little pond, which is the home to many varieties of wildfowl. After a short distance the road begins to run alongside the River Irvine. It then begins to wind uphill away from the river to a road junction at about 5 km out. Here carry straight on up the hill for a further 800m to a T-junction, and turn right following this undulating road into Moscow, 3.2 km further on. In Moscow, when the crossroads

INFORMATION

Distance: 24.1 km (15 miles), circular route.

Map: OS Landranger, sheet 70.

Start and finish: Car park off Wallace Street, Galston.

Terrain: This route is very hilly and not recommended for the inexperienced or unfit cyclist.

Refreshments: Various places in Galston and Newmilns.

Barr Castle, Galston.

with the A719 is reached, turn right on to this road. Although this is an A-class road, it is seldom very busy. However, care should be taken nevertheless, for there will certainly be fast-moving traffic using it. After only 2.4 km, however, it's goodbye to this road. Here turn left on to a minor road marked by a blue sign with B&B and Whatriggs on it. This road winds up a shallow hill for a little over 800m to a junction, at which point carry straight on. This road can be considered one of the best cycling roads in the area. Follow it down into a beautiful wooded valley and over a narrow bridge. Just south of here lie the ruins of Loudoun Castle, tragically burned down in 1941. It was first built as a tower house in the sixteenth century, and then lavishly turned into a grand mansion in the eighteenth century when it was the home of the Campbells, the Earls of Loudoun. In 1647 John Campbell, the first Earl, together with the Earl of Lanark and the Earl of Lauderdale, visited Charles I while the King was imprisoned in Carisbrooke Castle on the Isle of Wight. There they signed the 'Engagement' whereby the Scottish Lords promised the King military assistance in return for his agreement to establish Presbyterianism in England within three years. Ironically, less than 40 years later a group of Covenanters was imprisoned in the castle. The local men from Newmilns made a successful rescue attempt, setting the castle on fire as they made their escape.

The Loudoun Estate is now a Castle Park with many facilities, such as a museum, woodland walks and nature trails, and there is much to keep the children occupied. Access to the estate is off the A719, just after the roundabout north of Galston.

At the next junction turn left and cycle uphill for a little over 1.6 km past Loudoun Mains. Stop for a while to admire the beautiful views over the Irvine valley below, and also the hills further south, for they are splendid. After you pass East Head Farm, another road junction is reached. Turn right and follow the road steeply downhill past the Dry Ski Slope into Newmilns.

Newmilns became a Burgh of Barony in 1491. Its old Townhouse, built in 1739 in the traditional Scottish style with bellcote crownsteps and forestairs, is now the information centre. As with Darvel and its westerly neighbour Galston, Newmilns grew with the cotton and coalmining industries.

At the bottom of this hill the A71 is reached. Turn left here and then immediately right again into Brown Street. I suggest once again you dismount and continue on foot.

The Townhouse at Newmilns.

On entering Brown Street, go along this to its end. Here take the left-hand road which sweeps uphill and over a bridge, and then carry on up this hill, which is very steep in places, for almost 2.4 km. (To allay your worst fears, however, the very steep gradients are over short distances—although one is of the order of 1 in 7.)

Once again there are fine views to be seen when you reach the top, especially of the other side of the Irvine valley from whence you came.

At the next road junction, carry straight on and begin the descent back into Galston. This next section of road has many junctions, which are to be navigated as follows: first, straight on; second, after a little under 800m, turn right; third, only a short distance further on, turn left; fourth, now within Galston, turn right into Cessnock Road, which becomes Station Road; fifth, turn right into Wallace Street and thence back to the start of the route.

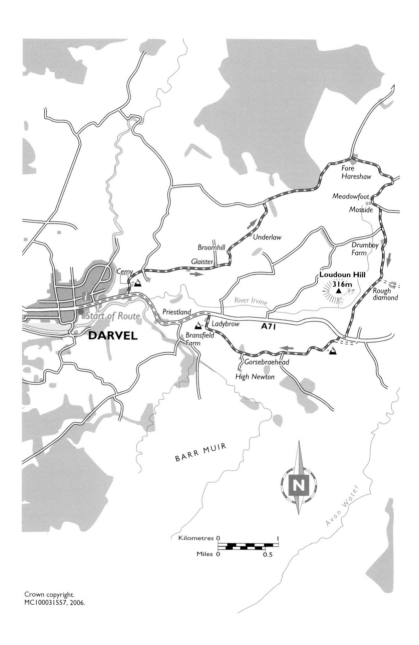

Fore
Hareshaw

Meadowfoot

Mosside

Underlaw

Broomhill

Drumboy
Farm

Glaister

Cemy

**Loudoun Hill
316m**

Rough
diamond

River Irvine

Priestland

Start of Route

Ladybrow

A71

DARVEL

Bransfield
Farm

Gorsebraehead

High Newton

BARR MUIR

N

Avon Water

Kilometres 0   1
Miles 0   0.5

DARVEL AND ITS SURROUNDS

Darvel was a planned town built at the beginning of the nineteenth century, which grew because of the linen industry and then coalmining. The weaving industry was revolutionised in 1876 when Alexander Morton introduced the power loom into the mills of the town and set up the manufacture of lace. Today many of the mills are still in existence, but only for the manufacture of knitwear.

In Hastings Square there is a bust of Alexander Fleming, the famous bacteriologist, who was born on a farm just outside the town. In 1928 he discovered the first antibiotic, penicillin, which was a giant step forward for medical science.

From the car park at East Mains Street, turn right and follow this busy trunk road to the outskirts of the town. Just past George Young Drive, the entrance to a housing estate, the small unclassified road veers off to the left. Take this road. It immediately rises uphill steeply, but not for long: for after passing the cemetery less than 400m along, the road flattens out.

After about 1.5 km, carry straight on at a crossroads up a slight incline, which continues gently rising for 2.4 km. At just over the 4 km point there is a road junction; turn right and continue uphill past the southern extremity of Whitelee Forest. After 6.4 km a series of three road junctions follow each other in fairly quick succession: first turn right, then 800m further on turn right again, and at the last of this series, a short distance more, carry straight on.

There is now a splendid view of the 316m-high Loudoun Hill. This is a volcanic plug which was scoured by glacial movement into a crag and tail formation. The Romans built a large garrison on

INFORMATION

Distance: 16.1 km (10 miles), circular route.

Map: OS Landranger, sheet 71.

Start and finish: Car park off East Mains Street, Darvel.

Terrain: Generally undulating with short stretches of steeper hills.

Refreshments: Various places in Darvel.

Cycling along the route.

Loudoun Hill, and from this vantage point they could control the local Celtic tribes who lived around the area. Under this hill is the site of a minor battle of the Wars of Independence. It was here, in 1307, that Robert the Bruce defeated the English under the command of the Earl of Pembroke. It is also interesting to note that the other great Scottish hero of the Wars of Independence,

William Wallace, was also involved in a skirmish here, against the same foe, some years before.

Loudon Hill.

At just over 8 km, as the road begins its descent back down towards the A71, there is a very tight double bend to negotiate, so care should be taken here.

At the junction with the A71 turn right and follow this main road for about 300m to where an entrance to a quarry is located. Turn left here and pass the quarry entrance, and just beyond this a minor road begins. Take care here, for the road surface at this quarry entrance is very rough indeed. Follow this very picturesque and quiet road for almost 3.2 km to where it once again joins the main road. The day I cycled this road I was escorted part of the way by hares, who had no difficulty in winning their race against this sluggish cyclist. Turn left and rejoin the main A71 and follow it, downhill, through the small village of Priestland and on to Darvel, 800m further on.

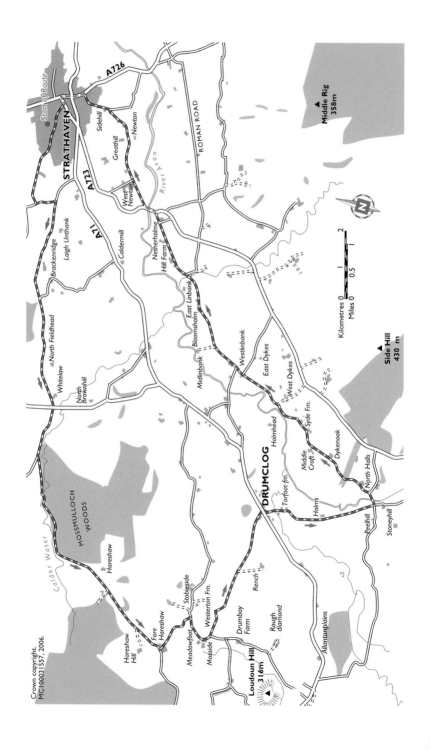

STRATHAVEN TO DRUMCLOG

INFORMATION

Distance: 24.1 km (15 miles), circular route.

Map: OS Landranger, sheet 71.

Start and finish: Car park off Glasgow Road, Strathaven.

Terrain: Generally mildly undulating.

Refreshments: Various places in Strathaven.

Strathaven, its name meaning wide valley of the Avon Water, is a small picturesque market town which has managed to hold on to its traditional character. The area around Strathaven has supported settlements of people for over 2,500 years and has always been easily accessible by visitors from the south. Some of these visitors were welcome; others much less so. The Romans were early visitors to the area, and one of their military roads ran from Carstairs through Sandford, just to the south of Strathaven, to Loudoun Hill.

In the town the Boo-Backet Bridge (which means highly arched) is reckoned by some to have been built in Roman times. Others tend to think, and I agree with them, that this bridge was built much later, probably in medieval times, at the site of the original Roman bridge.

Not much seems to be known about the family who became the feudal Lords of Avondell during the time of the reign of David I, but by the early fifteenth century it was in the hands, possibly through marriage, of the powerful Douglas family. There must have been some form

The Boo-Backet Bridge in Strathaven.

of keep in the area dating from the fourteenth century, and it's very possible it would have stood on the same site as the castle that can be seen today. This castle was built by Lord Avondell, but it was seldom lived in and was eventually allowed to fall into disrepair. There is a legend associated with the castle. A lord of the castle was so incensed by his wife's infidelity that he had her bricked up within the cavity of a wall, but had the 'generosity'

The old Town Mill, now an arts complex, in Strathaven.

to include a last meal of bread and water to be put in with her. Later, in the nineteenth century, bones were discovered when part of a wall fell down. It is not recorded if a plate and a cup were found next to the remains.

Next door to the castle is the town's mill, which was built by the Duke of Hamilton in 1650 for the local people to have their corn ground. It was used as a mill until 1966, latterly for grinding oatmeal. It was taken over by the town's Arts Guild in the 1970s and refurbished as a theatre and arts complex.

There is also a fine museum in Strathaven called the John Hastie Museum. John Hastie, who was a local grocer living at the end of the nineteenth century, bequeathed the money to build a park and museum for the good of the residents of Strathaven.

The route begins at the car park off Glasgow Road. Set off west past the boating pond into Threestanes Road, turn left here and follow this road until it joins Lethame Road. Here turn right into Lethame Road, which takes you out of the town and on to an unclassified road. Follow this road for 1.6 km until you come to a road junction. Here turn left, and then after only a short distance turn right at the next junction.

Close to this road is the site of the Battle of Drumclog, where, in 1679, 250 poorly armed Covenanters defeated a troop of the King's Dragoons led by John Graham of Claverhouse.

After 4 km a crossroads is reached. Carry straight on here to a fork in the road and go left, continuing on to the next junction a further 4 km away, and turn left again at Fore Hareshaw. Carry on now to the next junction only a short distance away, and this time turn right. On now another short distance to yet another junction, and this time carry straight on (keeping to the left) and after 2.4 km the little village of Drumclog is reached.

Drumclog was too small to have been shown on General Roy's map of Scotland in the eighteenth century, so the small collection of buildings that forms this hamlet must be fairly recent. However, at the edge of the village of Torfoot, Roman coins were found in 1806 when drains were being dug. Also, to the south of the village at Peel Farm, an Iron Age settlement has been excavated.

In 1912 Drumclog Memorial Kirk was built in remembrance of the nearby battle. Within this church is a stained-glass window depicting the Covenanters, and a replica of their banner is hung in the chancel. (The original is held in the John Hastie Museum.)

Cross the A71 and head down the B745 for 2.4 km to the first crossroads. Here turn left, still on this B-class road, and cross the bridge that spans the Glengaven Water. A few metres further on at the next road junction, take the minor road on the left. Carry on along this picturesque road, which is one of the most tremendous cycling roads I have come across anywhere, for the next 6.4 km to the junction with the A723. At this point turn left, cross the bridge over the Avon Water and turn immediately right and head uphill for 400m. When this road enters Strathaven it becomes Newton Road. At the end of Newton Road, turn left into Todshill Street. Then cross Kirk Street into Main Street, which joins Common Green, at the end of which carry straight on into Lethame Road, where there is an entrance to John Hastie Park. From here, it is only a few metres to the car park where the route began. (Please remember to dismount and walk within John Hastie Park.)

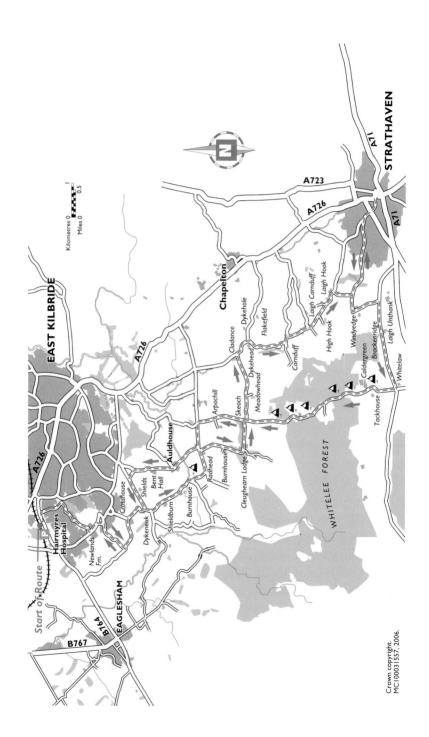

EAST KILBRIDE TO STRATHAVEN

East Kilbride is Scotland's first post-war 'New Town'. Founded in 1947, it is now the sixth largest town in the country. At its heart, however, is the charming old village, which still retains its original character. Most of the buildings in the village date from the seventeenth and eighteenth centuries, but in fact there has been a settlement here since medieval times. During the seventeenth century the people of this district were staunch Covenanters, and many men from East Kilbride parish fought at the Battle of Bothwell Brig. The banner they carried into battle was known as 'The Kilbryde Flag'.

One of the many interesting buildings in the village is the Montgomery Arms, a seventeenth-century coaching inn. In front stands a large rectangular stone with steps up one side, the 'Loupin on Stane'. This was there to help those who had perhaps taken too much drink, to get back on their horses.

The people living around East Kilbride are fortunate to be living in what can be described as a cyclists' paradise. There is a wonderful network of very quiet and picturesque minor roads throughout this area. These can be used, by all the family, for cycling in relative safety. Although I have selected specific routes in this district, you will find that once you are familiar with this unique network of roads, many different routes can be devised, allowing hours of cycling pleasure. These minor roads are seldom used by motor vehicles, but of course they are still part of the public road system, and cyclists should take care and be mindful of any vehicles which may be travelling along them.

INFORMATION

Distance: 41.8 km (26 miles), circular route.

Map: OS Landranger, sheets 64 and 71.

Start and finish: Hairmyres Railway Station car park off Eaglesham Road, East Kilbride.

Terrain: This route is very hilly, but only in the latter stages. I shall therefore also describe shorter and less hilly alternatives.

Refreshments: Various places in Strathaven.

The Loupin on Stane.

This route begins at Hairmyres Station car park. Hairmyres is one of the ancient boundaries of Kilbride, marked by a Celtic cross which can still be seen today in the grounds of Hairmyres Hospital. Turn left and carry on along Eaglesham Road, past Hairmyres Hospital, for almost 400m. Take care here, for this can be a busy road. Turn right into Windward Road, then immediately right again into Westport. (Alternatively, as Westport runs parallel to Eaglesham Road, cyclists can access it from the footpath at the eastern end, which directly links Eaglesham Road, and then take the first right into Dunedin Drive.) From here, turn left and carry on all the way along Dunedin Drive to the junction with Mossneuk Road and turn right.

Continue along Mossneuk Road to Wellesley Crescent and turn left. Carry on along the Crescent for about 300m until a formal footpath is reached on the left. Take this footpath for a short distance to a

Speeding cyclist.

junction of paths, turn left and within a few metres turn right, and after only a few metres more this footpath joins Eden Grove. Carry on uphill to Eden Drive, at the end of which turn left into Greenhills Road. After passing Newlandsmuir Road, cross over Greenhills Road and down a pedestrian ramp on the right into Newlands Road, past Londsdale Farm, following this road all the way to a T-junction. As you cycle down this road you will see that the town ends and the countryside begins. Here starts the series of roads featured both in this route and the next.

At the junction turn left, following the cycle signs to Strathaven, and keep going as the road winds uphill. Lickprivick Castle would have been near here. Alas, however, there is no trace of it left today. It belonged to the Lickprivick family, who were appointed Sergeants and Coroners of Kilbride by John Comyn in 1290, and later conspired, with Comyn, against Robert the Bruce.

After 1.6 km a T-junction is reached; here turn right, following signs for Auldhouse. After a few metres take the left fork and go on past Burnhouse Farm. After 2.4 km another T-junction is reached, which is signed for Auldhouse to the left. Turn right here, and then quickly take the left fork up a steep hill for a short distance, and after passing Raehead Farm turn right at the next junction. This road continues for 1.6 km, then turns at right angles when it passes Cleughearn Lodge. Bear left here and continue on to the crossroads, at which you carry straight on. This stretch of road has sheep farms on both sides, and at Meadowhead Farm you may see some Jacob's sheep. The next junction is at Cladance, where my main route turns right. However, for those who would like an easier route, turn left at this road junction and follow the road for 1.6 km to the next junction. Here turn left and follow the signs for Auldhouse. When this hamlet is reached, carry straight on, following signs for East Kilbride along this undulating road for almost 1.2 km, and then turn left. After 400m, turn left again. After a further 1.2 km, turn right on to the road which is signed for Jackton. Cycle another 1.6 km and you will reach a crossroads: here turn right (opposite the road which is signed for North and South Allerton). This is now the road on which you left the bounds of East Kilbride at the beginning of the route, so take the same route, in reverse, back to Hairmyres Station. This route is 16.5 km long and is predominantly flat.

Back to the main route: after turning right at the

next T-junction less than 800m further on, follow this road as it climbs gradually through moorland for over 1.6 km, before it starts downhill towards Strathaven. Along this stretch of road, which continues for 4.8 km, there are three road junctions: fork right at two of them and turn right at the third. Here there are good views over Lanarkshire, with Tinto Hill clearly visible to the south.

Carry on along this road for 400m to where a T-junction is reached and turn left. Follow this road downhill into Strathaven, where it becomes Lethame Road. At the end of Lethame Road, where it joins Townhead Street, carry straight on into Common Green, which is the picturesque centre of this charming town (see Route 17). The outward part of this journey is 19.3 km.

After you have explored the town and perhaps taken some refreshment, the way out of Strathaven is by the same way you came in, that is, back up Lethame Road. At the point where you joined the road which became Lethame Road, the main route carries straight on. This is also where the second alternative route begins: simply turn right and follow the same route taken in the outward journey to the junction at Cladance. At this point follow the easier route described above, until Hairmyres Railway Station car park is once again reached. This alternative, although it is not any shorter than taking the main route, avoids the steepest gradients encountered on it.

Back once more to the main route. Having gone straight on at the junction, carry on 400m to the next one and turn left. This minor road winds downhill for another 400m to a T-junction, where a right turn is made in the direction of Darvel. This road climbs very gradually for some 4 km until a crossroads is reached. Here turn right, back towards East Kilbride.

This road, which climbs some 90m over 4 km,

starts gently enough, but as it nears the summit and Whitelee Forest, it gets very steep in places. I would not recommend this route to families with children or to the less fit, unless you are prepared to walk at times along this 3.2 km stretch. Whitelee Forest is a modern commercial pine forest which was planted on the moorland. Long ago this area would also have been covered by trees, for it was once part of the Caledonian Forest, which covered a large area of Scotland.

Cows in the meadow.

If you are fit enough to cycle or are prepared to dismount and walk, then the view that awaits you at the summit is worth the climb. There is an incredible view over East Kilbride and other Lanarkshire towns, Glasgow, the Campsie Fells and Ben Lomond, and the Firth of Clyde as far as the Isle of Arran. In fact one can see, in a single vista, all the areas covered in the 25 routes of this book.

Once over the summit, the road begins to descend towards East Kilbride, passing straight across a crossroads en route. Care should be taken on this steep descent, for dangerously high speeds can be achieved very rapidly. At the end of this road, turn left and quickly pass one junction before turning right at the next, following the sign for Auldhouse. After 800m Auldhouse is reached. This sleepy little hamlet has an attractive old-world pub called the Auldhouse Inn, used as the scene of many television productions.

At Auldhouse, turn left past Auldhouse Primary School and carry on, following the signs for East Kilbride. Keep to this undulating road for almost 1.2 km, then turn left. After 400m turn left again. After a further 1.2 km turn right on to the road which is signed for Jackton. Within 1.6 km a crossroads is reached. Turn right opposite the road which is signed for North and South Allerton. This is now the road by which you left East Kilbride at the beginning of the route, so follow the same route, in reverse, back to Hairmyres Station.

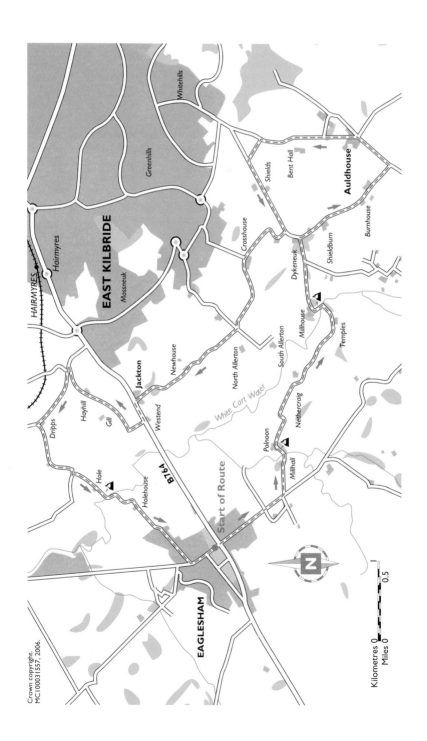

Kilometres 0
Miles 0
0.5

EAGLESHAM TO JACKTON

Eaglesham is a village with a very long history. It was the original home of the Montgomeries, Anglo-Norman knights, who had been granted land by Walter Fitzalan in these parts. Sir Hugh Montgomerie was later to serve Scotland valiantly at the Battle of Otterburn (Chevy Chase) in 1388. There is no trace of the Montgomeries' castle left at Eaglesham, for it was considered to be a ruin even in the eighteenth century.

The village lies at the edge of the lonely moorlands which were the scene of so many events in Covenanting times, with their network of remote, almost hidden paths. It was here that, after worshipping in the open air at a conventicle, the Covenanters could melt away into the moorland mists and escape the bloody attentions of Graham of Claverhouse, Grierson of Lagg or Turner, with their hellish crew of dragoons, who scoured these parts in murderous pursuit of the rebels.

The village underwent great changes in 1769 when the tenth Earl of Eglinton had the old village demolished and a new planned village built in its place. The new village was constructed in the form of a letter 'A' and is a striking example of Scottish domestic architecture of the time. When the village

INFORMATION

Distance: 14.5 km (9 miles), circular route.

Map: OS Landranger, sheet 64.

Start and finish: Gilmour Street, Eaglesham.

Terrain: Fairly flat with undulating stretches.

Refreshments: Various places in Eaglesham and the Auldhouse Inn, Auldhouse.

The village green, Eaglesham.

The Eglinton Arms,
Eaglesham.

was built, the houses had thatched roofs, but these
have all been replaced by slate. The two streets that
form the diagonals of the 'A' are Polnoon Street
and Montgomerie Street, and, with the large common between, the shape of the letter is still clearly
visible on a map. Today, this extremely pleasant
village, with its eighteenth-century coaching inn,
the Eglinton Arms, has been listed by government
as being of architectural and historical interest and
has become a Conservation Area, with most of the
buildings having been refurbished.

Leave Eaglesham by Strathaven Road, and after
almost 800m turn left at the junction signposted
for Strathaven. This road carries on downhill
and across the bridge over the Ardoch Burn, a
tributary of the White Cart Water. It then continues along this generally undulating road for
almost 3.2 km to another bridge, which this time
spans the upper reaches of the White Cart Water
itself. Almost immediately beyond this a short
but fairly steep hill has to be climbed before you
reach the next junction 800m beyond. Here turn
right at this 3-way junction and climb uphill again
for a short distance through the pleasant farming

countryside of Craigend and Harelaw farms, continuing along a road bounded by high hedges to the next road junction. Here turn right and follow the Strathaven Road uphill. After 1.6 km, carry straight on past a road on the right and take the next junction on the left, continuing for just over 800m to the hamlet of Auldhouse.

As in Route 18, at Auldhouse turn left past Auldhouse Primary School and keep following signs for East Kilbride along this undulating road for almost 1.2 km, at which point turn left. After 400m, turn left again. After a further 1.2 km, turn right on to the road which is signed for Jackton. Cycle along this road to Jackton, where it joins the B764, and turn left. After only a few hundred metres, turn right into the very narrow Hayhill Road. Take care making this manoeuvre, for the B764 is, very often, busy with traffic.

Once on the 3m-wide Hayhill Road the route becomes very quiet again. After 1.6 km, turn left. This road winds gently uphill for about 800m to the next junction, at which point turn left. About 800m further on, take the left fork and continue to a ford which crosses the White Cart Water once again. After the ford has been crossed, the road climbs quite steeply up to the beginning of Eaglesham, entering the village at Holehouse Road, at the top of which it joins Gilmour Street.

Speeding through Eaglesham.

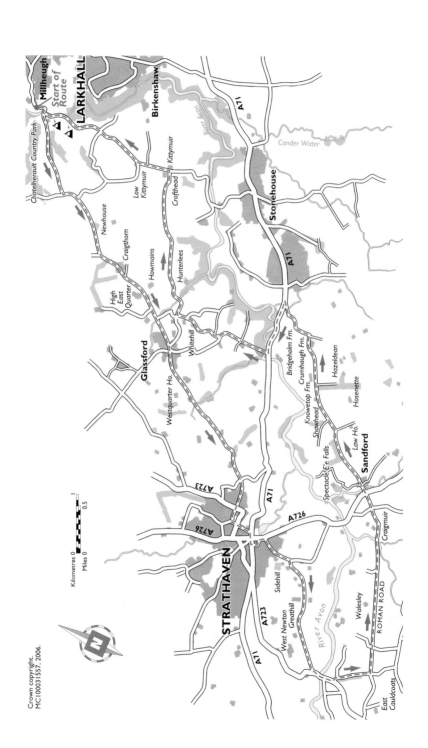

Crown copyright.
MC10003I557, 2006.

Kilometres 0
Miles 0   0.5

Chatelherault Country Park

Millheugh
Start of
Route

LARKHALL

Birkenshaw

River Avon

A71

Cander Water

Kittymuir
Low
Kittymuir
Crofthead

Newhouse

Craigthorn

Howmains

Hunterlees

Stonehouse

A71

High
East
Quarter

Whitehill

Glassford

Westquarter Ho.

Bridgeholm Fm.
Crumhaugh Fm.
Knowetop Fm.

Hazeldean

Hosenette

Shawhead

Low Ho.

Sandford

Spectacle E'e Falls

A723

A71

A726

STRATHAVEN

A723

A71

Sidehill

West Newton
Greathill

River Avon

Walesley

ROMAN ROAD

Craigmuir

East
Cauldcoats

LARKHALL TO STRATHAVEN

This route starts from Larkhall railway station. This railway line was reopened from Hamilton to Larkhall at the end of 2005, and is part of the Milngavie to Larkhall railway. This in turn is part of Greater Glasgow rail network, the second largest suburban rail network in the UK.

Turn right out of the station on to Commercial Road, and at the end of this turn right into McNeil Street. This road soon becomes Millheugh Brae; at the bottom of which turn left on to Millheugh. From here turn right, heading uphill. The road winds round past the Applebank Inn to a bridge which crosses the Avon Water. (It is worth noting, at this point, that once the bridge has been crossed there is a road off to the right leading to Chatelherault Country Park, where riverside paths form a direct off-road link to Strathclyde Park.) At the east end of the bridge, carry straight on uphill, fairly steeply, for a short distance before continuing less steeply for another 800m. At a T-junction turn left, and cycle along this fairly flat road for 1.6 km, until it starts to rise again quite steeply for a time. Pause here for a while and look back over a panoramic view of Lanarkshire. After just over 4.5km, the road comes into Glassford by the roundabout at Jackson Street. Here, turn right into Millar Street.

The small village of Glassford, set amongst rich agricultural land, has for many centuries had its roots in farming, although in the eighteenth-century it became a centre for hand-loom weaving. Support for the Covenant was strong here, and many local men fought at Bothwell Bridge and Drumclog to defend their faith.

INFORMATION

Distance: 30 km (18.5 miles), circular route.

Map: OS Landranger, sheets 64 and 71.

Start and finish: Larkhall Railway Station. The station has a car park for those arriving by car.

Terrain: mainly undulating, with short stretches of steep hills.

Refreshments: Various places in Larkhall and Strathaven.

New railway station at Larkhall.

The ruins of St Ninian's Church.

At the ruins of St Ninian's Parish Church there is a memorial to William Gordon of Earlston, who was shot by dragoons while on his way to fight at Bothwell Brig.

At the end of Millar Street, the road continues downhill to Strathaven, arriving in the town at Commercial Road. Turn left into North Street, which joins Castle Street. At the end of this is a multiple junction. Here turn left into Todshill Street. After passing Station Road, turn right into Newton Road, which takes you out of Strathaven again. At the next junction fork right and continue for about 1.5 km to the 'Give Way' sign at the junction with the A723. Here turn left across the bridge over the Avon Water. Join this quiet A-class road for a little over 400m to where a minor road goes off to the left. Take this road as it climbs uphill, fairly steeply in places, until it joins the Roman road at a crossroads 800m further on. Here turn left and follow this typical Roman road, which is straight but undulating, for 2.4 km. At this point, maps suggest that the Roman road would have continued in a straight line while the modern road meanders for another 800m before it joins the A726. The route crosses this main road and continues on the minor road on the other side into Sandford.

Rough path through Spectacle E'e Mill.

Sandford is a pleasant little village, with the Kype Water flowing past and its rows of single-storey cottages with their gardens ablaze with colour in summer. It has recently been given the status of a conservation village. Close to the village is the famous beauty spot known as the Spectacle E'e Falls. This beautiful waterfall took its name from a local tale of love and revenge. It is said that in the eighteenth century, the miller of Overhall Mill had a beautiful daughter who was loved by a local Sandford lad, but the miller would not allow his daughter to have anything to do with him. One night, out of spite, the lad climbed on to the thatched roof of the mill and fixed a pair of spectacles to the thatch. The next day, when the sun rose, the spectacles set fire to the roof. By the time the local people got to the blaze and put the fire out, only the four walls remained. When the mill was rebuilt it was henceforth known as the Spectacle E'e Mill, and the nearby waterfalls known as the Spectacle E'e Falls. Access to the ruined mill and the falls is along the little road by the river on the left, immediately after crossing the green metal bridge. However, if you want to visit this beauty spot do it on foot, leaving your bikes at Sandford.

Spectacle E'e Falls.

From Sandford the road continues uphill steadily for 800m. The road undulates fairly steeply up and down to where it joins the A71, 3 km further on. Turn left on to this main road, cycle along it for a little less than 800m and turn right on to the Glassford Road. Cross over the Avon Water by Glassford Bridge, where the road begins to climb again. The climb is constant for 2 km, sometimes gradual and sometimes steep, until it reaches a crossroads. Just before this crossroads you will see the ruins of the old St Ninian's Parish Church. Turn right at the crossroads and follow this road for 2.4 km to where a T-junction is reached, and here turn left. Head down this road for 400m to another T-junction at Low Kittymuir Farm, and turn right following the sign for Larkhall.

This minor road passes under a dismantled railway before beginning its descent back to Millheugh. A word of warning: take care not to go too fast down the steep hill, which at times has a gradient of 1 in 7, for there are corners to negotiate. This road ends at the eastern end of the bridge over the Avon Water. Just cross this bridge again and retrace your route back to Larkhall railway station.

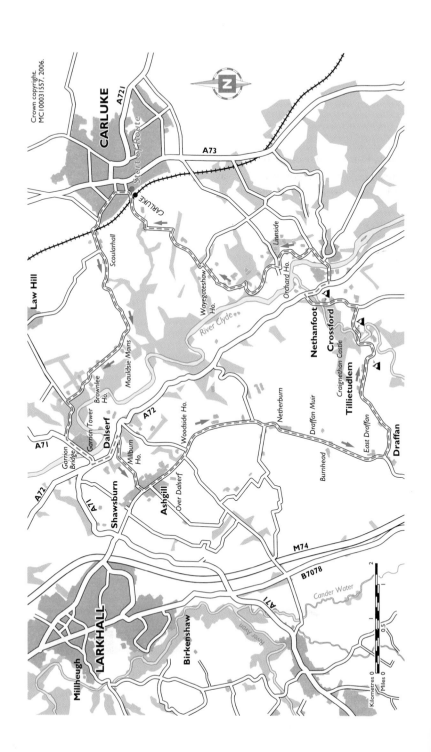

Crown copyright.
MC100031557, 2006.

CARLUKE TO CROSSFORD

Turn right out of the station on to Station Road, cycle for a few hundred metres to Kirkton Avenue and turn left. At the end of Kirkton Avenue, turn left down Clyde Street to the roundabout and then carry straight on. Although this is only a C-class road it can be quite busy, but not busy enough to concern an experienced cyclist. Keep going all the way downhill for 4 km, an almost completely effortless and a very exhilarating run, to the junction with the B7011. Here turn left and once again wind downhill to the junction with the A71, 800m further on. Turn left on to the roundabout formed recently by the construction of a new road bridge across the River Clyde alongside the original Garrion Bridge. Take the junction at the west side of the roundabout and follow the A72 for 800m to Dalserf. At Dalserf turn right on to a minor road. This is an awkward junction which turns back on itself. I therefore recommend that you dismount and re-mount when you are safely on the minor road. (At this point it is possible to shorten this

INFORMATION

Distance: 28 km (17.5 miles), circular route.

Map: OS Landranger, sheets 65 and 72.

Start and finish: Carluke Railway Station.

Terrain: Undulating with stretches of very steep hills. Not suitable for inexperienced or unfit cyclists.

Refreshments: Various places in Crossford and Carluke.

Dalserf Parish Church.

cycle run, thus avoiding the most severe hill on the route. This is done by continuing south along the A72 to Crossford, which reduces this route to 17.7 km and gives the choice of doing the second part another time. A word of warning: this road can be very busy, particularly at weekends.

Opposite this road is a little road which makes its way down to the tiny hamlet of Dalserf, where at the end of its row of pretty cottages stands the beautiful and historic Dalserf Parish Church, founded in 1655. It is here that John Macmillan (1669-1753) is buried. As described on his monument, he was the Covenanter of Covenanters. After being ordained in 1701 he joined the Cameronian movement, which was founded by Richard Cameron, known as the Lion of the Covenant. Macmillan led the movement after Cameron's death, rejecting the settlement of the church and vowing to continue to fight for the right of the Covenant. The Cameronian movement retained its identity, and finally was instrumental in setting up the Free Church of Scotland in 1876. The Cameronian Regiment was also raised from this group.

This road winds uphill very steeply at first, then less steeply, and after 800m the top of the hill is

Craignethan Castle.

reached. Here the view over the Clyde Valley is magnificent. Soon this road comes into the small village of Ashgill at Millburn Road. Here, if you turn right, it is less than 3.2 km into the heart of Larkhall.

Our route is to the left at this junction. Follow this road, through Netherburn, for 5 km. Here turn left at the road junction signed for Craignethan Castle. As the road turns east there are panoramic views over the Clyde Valley and the hills to the south of Lanarkshire. At the next junction turn left, still following signs for Craignethan Castle. The road then passes through the tiny hamlet of Tillietudlem, at the end of which is the entrance to Craignethan Castle.

Craignethan Castle was built in the 1530s for Sir James Hamilton. It was the last of the fortress residences to be built in Scotland. From its position high on top of a hill, protected on three sides by a steep escarpment, around which the Water of Nethan still meanders, it should have been an impenetrable fortress. This however was not the case; for the castle was sacked and laid waste before the end of the sixteenth century. Craignethan Castle is Sir Walter Scott's Tillietudlem Castle in *Old Mortality*.

Just after passing this entrance the road begins to descend at a gradient of 12 per cent, which is clearly signed at the top of the hill. Take care cycling down this hill, for there are some double bends to contend with *en route*, so keep the speed down. Perhaps even walk! At the bottom of this hill the road passes through a farmyard and then over a bridge spanning the River Nethan. At this point there is a good view of Craignethan Castle over to the left. Here the opposite of the old proverb is true, for in this case what comes down must go up. The road rises as steeply, for 800m, back uphill as previously it descended. Once again it may be advisable to walk this stretch. At the end of this

Typical of what might be seen at the Bird of Prey Centre.

hill a road junction is reached. Here turn left and begin the descent to Crossford. Care should also be taken on this descent, with an effort being made to keep the speed down. At the bottom of this hill turn right on to the A72 at the Tillietudlem Hotel and continue along this road for a few hundred metres to the B7056 Braidwood Road. Here turn left and carry on across the stone bridge that spans the River Clyde. On the other side on the right is the Clyde Valley Country Estate, where there are many attractions to interest the visitor, including a Narrow Gauge Railway, Birds of Prey Centre, Pony Trekking Centre and also a cafeteria. Continue along the B7056 for less than 800m to reach the

River Clyde at Crossford.

first steep incline, but this is only about 200m long. After this incline turn left on to the unclassified road signed for Waygateshaw. After 1.6 km on this pleasant road it starts to climb again at various gradients for 1.6 km. Some of these gradients are very steep indeed, but the very steep sections tend to be over short distances.

At the top of this hill is a road junction. Turn left and continue along this road for about 800m to the junction with an even more minor road. Down this minor road at Milton Head was the birthplace of Major General William Roy of the Royal Engineers. Born in 1726, he is best known for his preparation of the map of mainland Scotland known as the Duke of Cumberland's Map, which can be seen in the British Museum in London. This map was the forerunner of Ordnance Survey maps, which today are such a valuable asset to those wishing to venture into the countryside. He is also known for his research into the Roman occupation of Britain.

Carry on past this minor road to the next junction a few hundred metres further on and turn left. Follow this road over Jock's Burn, after which Carluke Railway Station is soon reached.

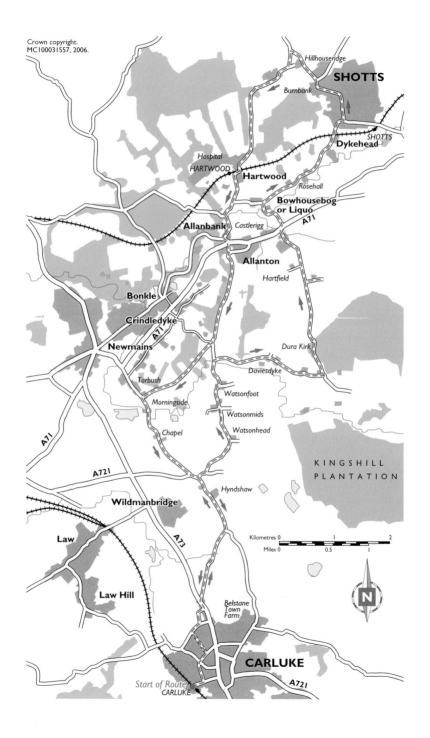

Crown copyright.
MC100031557, 2006.

SHOTTS

Hillhouseridge

Burnbank

SHOTTS

Dykehead

Hospital
HARTWOOD

Hartwood

Rosehall

Bowhousebog
or Liquo

A71

Allanbank Castlerigg

Allanton

Hartfield

Bonkle

Crindledyke

A71

Dura Kirk

Newmains

Daviesdyke

Torbush

Watsonfoot

Morningside

Watsonmids

Chapel

Watsonhead

KINGSHILL
PLANTATION

A71

A721

Hyndshaw

Wildmanbridge

A73

Law

Kilometres 0 1 2
Miles 0 0.5 1

Law Hill

Belstane
Town
Farm

CARLUKE

N

Start of Route
CARLUKE

A721

CARLUKE TO SHOTTS

The parish of Carluke was granted the status of Burgh of Barony by King Charles II in 1662, in favour of Captain Walter Lockhart of Kirktoune. However, the town that is seen today did not come into being until later.

On leaving the station car park, turn right on to Station Road and follow it for a few hundred metres, then turn left into Kirkton Avenue. At the end of the Avenue, cross Clyde Street, turn right into Kirk Street and then right once again into Kirk Road. Follow this road to the junction with Holm Street and turn left into Holm Street. At the junction with Douglas Street, Holm Street ends, but across the road a signed cycle path continues. This is what is left of Old Wishaw Road. Carry on down this cycle path to Weighhouse Road and turn right. Take the first on the left into Bothwell Road, then the third on the right into Stirling Road. This road is only a few metres long, and at the end of it there is another footpath leading to Airdrie Road. On this footpath you will have to dismount for a few metres. Cross over the busy Airdrie Road (the A73) into Castlehill Road. The route now continues along this road, into the countryside, for 1.5 km to a road junction. Here turn left and keep to this road, which has a short but steep uphill stretch. Turn right at the next junction, where there is a sign for North Lanarkshire Council.

You will see from the splendid views, as far as the Campsie Fells, that this area is generally very high, about 200m above sea level in fact. The quiet unclassified road meanders through picturesque fields and past large affluent farmhouses at regular intervals. After going under a disused railway bridge, there is a road junction, and here you turn right and head slowly uphill for 400m. In fact there are a few hills on this stretch, none of them particularly long or steep. Now the horizon is dominated

INFORMATION

Distance: 30.5 km (19 miles), circular route.

Map: OS Landranger, sheets 65 and 72.

Start and finish: Carluke Railway Station.

Terrain: Undulating with long flat stretches.

Refreshments: Various places in Carluke and Shotts.

Wind farm on Black Law.

by a large wind farm. At the next junction turn left and continue past the forest known as Kingshill Plantation and the ruins of Dura Kirk.

In 1740 an earlier church, the Moor Kirk of Cambusnethan, was built on this site, but that heather-roofed structure was replaced by the present building in 1780. However, this church fell into disrepair when the congregation moved to Bonkle, a few miles to the north, in 1843.

From here the countryside changes to open moorland. There are many signs of quarrying and a few spoil heaps dotted around, though the area is not unattractive. Soon begins the descent into the village of Allanton, where the A71 is reached. Cross this busy road, and 100m further, on the right you come to another minor road along which you continue.

Cycle down this pretty little road for 800m to the next road junction and turn right. If one turns left at this point, however, keeps on this road for less than 800m and turns left at the T-junction, joining up with the route again further on, this shortens the route by about 6.4 km. This shorter route is generally easy cycling. If you continue on the main route after turning right, the road begins to climb towards Shotts with short, fairly steep stretches from time to time. On entering Shotts this road becomes Rosehall Road, at the end of which it joins Shottskirk Road and Station Road. (Turn right down Station Road if you want to go to the railway station.) Turn left into Shottskirk Road, passing two streets on the left before coming to a 4-way junction. Here Shottskirk Road continues on the left out of Shotts and so does the route, passing the headquarters of the Central Scottish Countryside Trust. Turn left at the T-junction following the sign for Hartwood. After a short uphill stretch this road descends for almost 2.4 km, passing Murdostoun

View over Shotts.

Forest, into Hartwood. Once you are through this little village, the short-cut referred to earlier rejoins the main route. It may be useful to note that Hartwood also has a railway station with a park-and-ride facility.

Then, 200m past where the short-cut merges, is another junction. Here carry straight on, and after a further few hundred metres a T-junction is reached at Allanton. Turn left, and shortly the A71 is once more reached. At this point, dismount and cross this road to reach a footpath on the other side. Turn right, cycle up this footpath, and after 100m it joins a road-end called Mill Road. Very soon Mill Road comes to a T-junction, at which point veer right (do not turn hard right) and on out of the village. This little manoeuvre saves a 800m detour through Allanton. (The alternative route through Allanton is: turn left along the A71 for 200m or so, and then turn right into Coltness Avenue and follow this uphill and out of the village.) Follow this road for about 1.5 km to a 4-way junction. Here veer to the right (once again do not turn hard right). Carry on along this road for 1.6 km to Morningside and turn left at a T-junction there. Once out of this tiny hamlet the road begins to climb, sometimes fairly steeply, for 800m, when it levels out once again. A little further on, the road which was used on the first leg of the journey is passed on the left. Carry on for a further 2 km, now retracing the route already taken, to the next junction where a right turn is made. From here retrace this route back for 1.2 km, to where it joins the A72. Then continue, using the route in reverse through Carluke to the railway station.

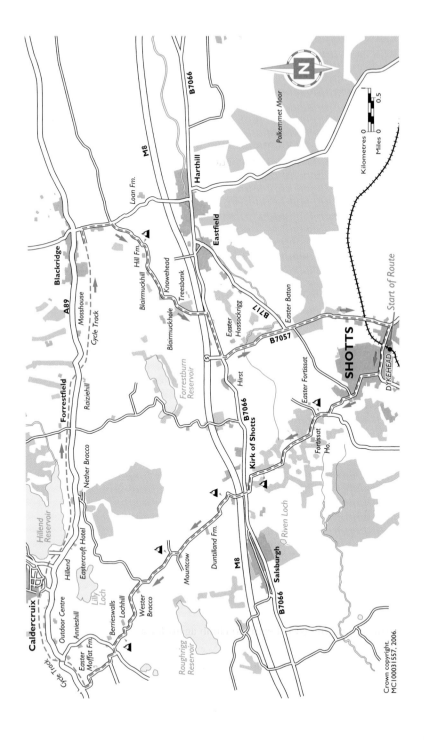

SHOTTS TO BLACKRIDGE

From Shotts Railway Station turn left and continue along Station Road, which after passing through the town centre becomes Shottskirk Road. Carry on uphill on Shottskirk Road, passing two streets on the left before coming to a 4-way junction. Here Shottskirk Road continues on the left out of Shotts, and so does the route. Passing the major junction on the right signposted to Harthill, continue for another 500m to the T-junction and turn right following the sign for Salsburgh. After passing the perimeter fence of HM Prison Shotts, the road begins to climb uphill, sometimes steeply for short distances, for 1.6 km until the summit, at 300m above sea level, is reached. On this incline after about 800m is the Fortissat Stone, or Covenanters' Stone, which is clearly visible as it protrudes out on to the road. This stone was used as a meeting place for conventicles by 40 Covenanters from Shotts parish. At the top of this hill, as a reward for the effort made to get up, there is a splendid view over West Lanarkshire and beyond.

INFORMATION

Distance: 32.2 km (20 miles), circular route.

Map: OS Landranger, sheet 65.

Start and finish: Shotts Railway Station car park.

Terrain: Mainly undulating, with short stretches of fairly steep hills.

Refreshments: Various places in Shotts, Plains, Caldercruix and Blackridge.

The Fortissat or Covenanters' Stone near Shotts.

After 800m the road begins to climb again for a short distance before making its descent down to Kirk o' Shotts. (This beautiful old parish church was built at the beginning of the nineteenth century and stands in a most imposing position.) A few hundred metres past the church the junction with the B7086 is reached. Here turn right, then almost immediately left and continue across the bridge, which spans the M8 motorway.

After crossing the motorway the road climbs steeply for 500m to where once more there is another incredible panoramic view all the way to Glasgow and beyond.

From here also there is a good view of Roughrigg Reservoir, a short distance to the west. In the next 2.4 km the road is very undulating, climbing gradually with three short sections of steep incline interspersed with short downhill stretches, until finally it reaches the summit. Almost at the top of this hill is the Blackhill Transmitter, which, with its near neighbour, Kirk o' Shotts, to the east, beams television signals to Central Scotland.

The road then descends for a little over 1.5 km to where a T-junction is located, at which turn left. After only 200m, at the next junction, turn right into Brownieside Road and start downhill once again. This road becomes Station Road Plains, where the Glasgow to Edinburgh cycle route runs in both directions.

Turn right here on to the Glasgow to Edinburgh cycle track and follow it for the next 13 km to Blackridge. Since this cycle route is built on the disused railway track bed of the Glasgow to Bathgate railway, and is well defined and signed along its length, it is not necessary to describe the route in detail. I will, however, point out the places of interest along the way.

Hillend Reservoir.

After 3.2 km Hillend Reservoir is reached. This is a particularly attractive area with a wooded backdrop on the other side of the

The Bedrock Bicycle.

loch. It is used by many anglers, who can be seen sitting on the banks, rod in hand, fishing at all times of the day during both summer and winter. This part of the cycleway is also used by many people enjoying a walk along the loch side.

Also along this stretch there are two sculptures: the first, called Calorman, depicts a fisherman with rod and line, and the second, called Bedrock Bicycle, is, as its name suggests, a bicycle of gigantic proportions.

Once Hillend Reservoir is passed, the route runs for about 10 km along this pleasant cycle path, from North Lanarkshire into West Lothian, to Blackridge. At Blackridge a bridge carrying the B718 is reached. Here take the ramp up on to this road, turn right and continue uphill to the edge of the village. A few metres past this point there is a minor road off to the right. Follow this very pleasant little road for about 3 km as it climbs south-west, sometimes steeply, towards the M8 motorway. After passing under the motorway, the T-junction with the B7066 is reached. Turn right and follow this road for just over 1 km to the next junction, at which point turn left on to the B7057. Now follow this road for about 3 km to a roundabout. Here turn right into Shotts, where after a short distance Shotts Railway Station is reached.

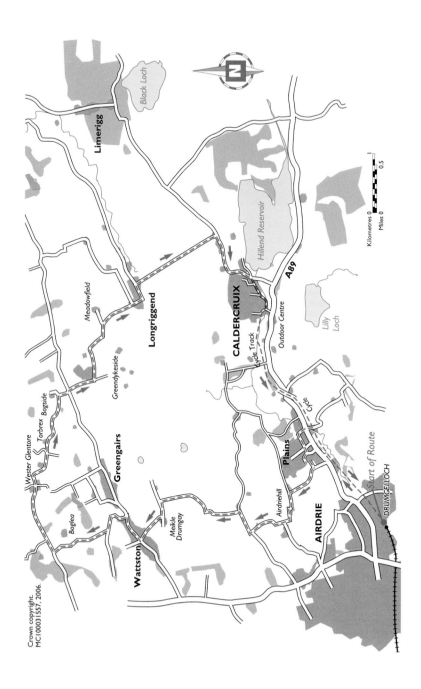

AIRDRIE TO LONGRIGGEND

I n the words of the local song:

Airdrie's a rer wee toon, so it is, so it is,
Airdrie's a rer wee toon.
It's better than Greenock, it's better than
  Troon,
Some people say it's better than Dunoon.

(Sung to the tune of: 'Who were you with last night, under the pale moonlight'.)

From this it is obvious that Airdrieonians have a certain pride in their town.

In 1996 the Glasgow to Edinburgh Cycle route (National Cycle Route 75) was completed, and this runs through both Coatbridge and Airdrie. The first part of our route from Drumgelloch Station to Plains is about 3 km long and uses part of NCN 75. Indeed on the return journey it also uses it from Caldercruix back to Drumgelloch Station. At Station Road, which cuts across the cycle path, turn left, and after about a hundred metres the junction with Main Road, which is also the A89, is reached. Cross this road into Northburn Street,

INFORMATION

Distance: 26.5 km (16.5 miles), circular route.

Map: OS Landranger, sheets 64 and 65.

Start and finish: Drumgelloch Railway Station car park.

Terrain: Mainly undulating with fairly flat stretches.

Refreshments: Various places in Plains and Caldercruix.

Cycling along NCN 75.

then left into Jarvie Avenue. Follow Jarvie Avenue around until it joins Wallace Street and turn left. At the next junction turn right into Bruce Street and then take the next street on the left, which is Annieshill View. At the end of this, turn right into Meadowhead Road and on out of Plains.

This minor road winds uphill, sometimes steeply, for 800m. This is the most severe climb that will be encountered on this route. At the top of the hill turn left. Follow this road, passing two junctions on the left, for about 2.4 km to a 3-way junction, and turn left into Darngavil Road. Continue along this road for another 2.4 km into Wattston. I confess that the scenery by this road, at the moment, is not very attractive, but the land is being rehabilitated by Central Scottish Countryside Trust. However, it is worthwhile tolerating this temporary blot, because after Wattston the scenery improves dramatically.

Once Wattston is reached, turn right on to the B803 in the direction of Greengairs. Travel through the village for 400m and then turn left on to a road known as Cameron Road. (This is the first on the left after the village has been passed.) Carry on around this road for 800m or so, and take the road off to the right known as Brackenknowe Road. Now, as I promised, the scenery is much better, with fine views across to Cumbernauld and the Kilsyth Hills beyond. The only warning I should give is that the road surface on this minor road is bad, so care should be taken here.

At the end of this road turn right, and follow this now extremely pleasant minor road, which, with the trees on both sides, although they are not poplars, I must say reminded me in places of France. After 800m the road continues past roads on the right and the left, then starts to climb in steps, sometimes quite steeply, for short distances, for another 800m.

Land prepared for forestry planting.

Another junction with the B803 is reached 1.6 km further on. Here turn left, and within a few metres right again, following the road signed for Longriggend Remand Centre. The road heads up-hill, and includes 100m of very steep climb, before passing the Remand Centre, after which it levels off for 800m. It starts to climb again gradually for a few hundred metres to where a road junction is reached, here following the road on to the small hamlet of Longriggend. Once over the humped-back railway bridge, the road turns at right angles, now called Main Street, through the small village. After 250m the junction with Telegraph Road is reached. Turn right on to Telegraph Road and cycle past the peat fields on either side to the junction with the B825. Right at the T-junction, carry on downhill to Caldercruix and turn right into the village at Main Street. Go along Main Street and over the old railway bridge, which now passes over the Glasgow to Edinburgh cycle track. Continue to the bottom of this street where you will see Longriggend and Meadowfield Church. Here on the west side of the church the access to the cycle track, NCN 75, is found. From here, go onto the cycle track and continue back in a westerly direction, for 5 km, to Drumgelloch Station.

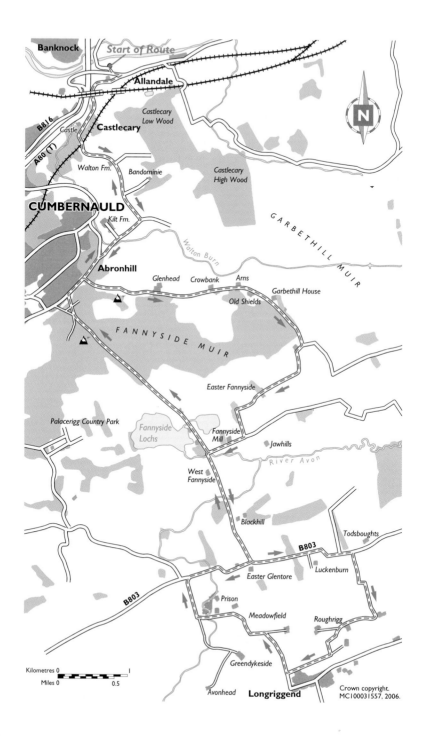

Banknock

Start of Route

Allandale

B816

Castle

Castlecary

A80 (T)

Castlecary
Low Wood

Walton Fm.

Bandominie

Castlecary
High Wood

CUMBERNAULD

Kilt Fm.

GARBETHILL MUIR

Abronhill

Walton Burn

Glenhead

Crowbank

Arns

Old Shields

Garbethill House

FANNYSIDE MUIR

Easter Fannyside

Palacerigg Country Park

Fannyside
Lochs

Fannyside
Mill

Jawhills

River Avon

West
Fannyside

Blackhill

Todsboughts

B803

Luckenburn

Easter Glentore

B803

Prison

Meadowfield

Roughrigg

Greendykeside

Kilometres 0   1

Miles 0   0.5

Avonhead

Longriggend

Crown copyright.
MC100031557, 2006.

CASTLECARY TO LONGRIGGEND

Castle Cary was built in 1473 by the Livingston family and is still standing today. Cary means fort, from the old word 'caer': Castle Cary therefore is the 'castle of the fort'. The original fort was Roman, and the castle was built re-using its stone.

The route begins at the Forth and Clyde Canal at Castlecary. Set off up the road from the canal bank, turn left on to the A80 access road and continue on to the junction with the B816. Turn right and almost immediately turn left on to Walton Road. This road winds round and under the viaduct which carries the main Glasgow to Edinburgh railway high above. The road then begins to climb fairly gradually for 1.6 km, passing Castle Cary. There are good views over Cumbernauld and the hills beyond from this road. After another 1.2 km, the road begins to wind uphill once again to where a T-junction is reached. Here turn left on to a fine modern road, but within only a few hundred metres turn left on to the road which is signed for Arns. This road immediately begins to climb fairly gradually once again for a short distance. The road continues almost flat and dead straight for 1.6 km and then gradually begins to wind uphill again for a short distance past the small cluster of houses which is Arns. This little minor road is a perfect road for cycling. On now past a radar mast, 400m

INFORMATION

Distance: 29 km (18 miles), circular route.

Map: OS Landranger, sheets 64 and 65.

Start and finish: From the canal at Castlecary. If driving to the beginning of this route at Castlecary, go along the B816 in the direction of Bonnybridge and then turn into the access road for the A80 in the direction of Glasgow. Halfway down this access road the canal access road is located on the right. There is no formal car park here, but the road is broad and there is room for a few cars to park quite comfortably.

Terrain: Fairly flat with two long, gradual hills.

Refreshments: 1.6 km (1 mile) east from Castlecary there is a restaurant and bar called Underwood Lockhouse.

Lock on the Forth and Clyde canal.

Underwood Lockhouse near Castlecary.

after which a T-junction is reached, where a right turn is made. It is interesting to note that there seem to be many birds of prey around this area and they offer a fine spectacle as they hunt for their daily meal.

Carry on now for 1.2 km to where the road passes straight through the yard of Easter Fannyside Farm. Take care here, as there is a road hump across the road in the farmyard, but it should not cause any harm to the cyclist. The countryside here is very pleasant, with Fannyside Lochs visible on the right. Soon afterwards keep right, and after passing Fannyside Mill carry on to a T-junction and turn left. There is now another very straight stretch of road, which continues, on the rise, for 1.6 km, to where it joins the B803. Here turn left and climb gradually uphill for 1.6 km. Take the second turning on the right, which is not signposted, on to another minor road.

Follow this picturesque country road for 3.2 km, as it meanders around a few bends and gradually uphill to where it joins the Longriggend Road, just at the beginning of the village itself. However, unless a shop is required, turn right and head away from Longriggend. After 2 km the road rises

steeply for 200 m as it passes Longriggend Remand
Centre before descending to the B803 once again.
Here turn right and continue along the B803 for
1.2 km to the road junction where the B803 was
joined some 8 km before.

Turn left back on to this minor road once again,
but this time carry straight on at the next junction. This road now passes between Fannyside
Lochs with a boat-yard on the left. The land which
borders the road in this vicinity is full of peat.
After 1.5 km the road then begins to descend
through the woods of Fannyside Muir, towards
Cumbernauld.

Cycling along the tow-path.

Just before entering Cumbernauld the descent
becomes steep, so take care here not to gather too
much speed. Soon a T-junction is reached. Here
turn right following the sign for Castlecary. After
800m, passing en route the Arns Road once again,
there is the junction of the road which was used
for the first leg of this route. Turn right on to this
road where it is signed for Castlecary and retrace
the route back to the Forth and Clyde Canal.

INDEX